"*Just Getting Started* encompasses the much-needed message that our Christ-like identities are obtainable with biblical truths and healthy self-care. Wendy has communicated the importance of this through her own unique life journey. This book will be an important resource to assist you if prayerfully processed and applied in your life."

Diane and Neal Arnold, marriage and family authors
and speakers; founders, The Family Collective

"*Just Getting Started* will help you unlock a greater vision of what is possible with God while challenging you to step into all God has for you. Wendy's candid testimonies will help you overcome self-doubt and fear of failure to achieve what matters—realizing the fullness of God's plan for your life."

Brandi Belt, healing evangelist, international speaker,
leadership coach; co-founder, Overflow Global Ministries

"Welcome to the realm of possibility! This wonderful book will stir you to dream anew, take old dreams off the shelf and equip you to identify and remove obstacles that have separated you from the future of your dreams! It's time to rise, SHINE—and impact your world!"

Vee Michelle Burkett, Ph.D., director,
Women in Ministry Network (WIMN)

"To pick up this book is to pick up the dreams deep within you that are waiting to declare, 'This is what I was created to do!' *Just Getting Started* is a masterpiece for all ages who desire to launch their dreams and step into all God has planned for them."

Cathie Harrison, c⸱ ⸱⸱⸱⸱⸱ ⸱⸱⸱ R.O.C. Church
Interr⸱

"Wendy Peter shares her life journey with refreshing authenticity and vulnerability. As you enter into her story, you'll see your own story unfold as God shines His light on areas of your life. This book is filled with personal examples, impactful Scripture, and steps to freedom. You'll begin to dream at new levels."

Rev. Ruth Hendrickson, pastor, mentor and conference
speaker; president, RHM International

"Wendy is a champion and encourager for releasing people to go after their dreams! While reading the introduction, I was captivated and stirred by her statement, 'I don't have any dreams left.' This book is a must-read for anyone whose dreams have been buried under the cares of life!"

Carol L. Koch, founder and director,
Children on the Frontline

"The world needs solutionaries—people inspired by God to bring much-needed change in our world. Through Wendy's book, you'll recognize that you are a solutionary—given purpose and dreams by God that can change our world for the better. And no, that's not exaggeration; it's truth—it's who you are. In this book you'll discover practical help and inspiration that will enable you to step up and be who you were created to be."

Lyn Packer, facilitator, New Zealand Prophetic Network

"With this book, Wendy provides both the tools and the inspiration to embark on a new dream or resurrect a dream that has fallen. Wendy skillfully imparts wisdom, hope and fresh passion throughout. If you feel stuck or need some fresh fire, start here. Love it!"

Vita Panico, teacher and intercessor;
author, *Gatekeepers Arise*

"Wendy writes with beauty, insight, maturity and humility, wraps it in a package of Holy Spirit and gives us just enough humor to make it relatable at any age. For all of us who think someone else holds the power to fulfill our dreams, Wendy shows us how to overcome and fulfill our purpose."

Duane and Tamara Siemens, lead pastors,
The Wave Church, Winnipeg, Manitoba

"*Just Getting Started* takes you on a journey to uncover the dreams that you never thought possible. Wendy has provided sage counsel and practical steps that take you from discovery to activation. Expect that your heart will be awakened to the more God has for you!"

Cindy Stewart, consultant and coach; author,
God's Dream for Your Life, Insights for an Abundant Life

"Courageous and always so encouraging, Wendy is the best leader your cheering squad can have! *Just Getting Started* makes you feel that anything is possible and you are ready to begin the adventure. Thank you for writing this, Wendy. Your insight and ability to help people process their dream is a gift to so many."

Helen Toews, author, *Jacob's Ladder,*
Heaven's Court, Emma's Corner

Just Getting Started

Just Getting Started

Stepping with Courage into God's Call for the NEXT STAGE OF LIFE

WENDY PETER

Chosen

a division of Baker Publishing Group
Minneapolis, Minnesota

© 2021 by Wendy Peter

Published by Chosen Books
11400 Hampshire Avenue South
Minneapolis, Minnesota 55438
www.chosenbooks.com

Chosen Books is a division of
Baker Publishing Group, Grand Rapids, Michigan

Printed in the United States of America

Library of Congress Cataloging-in-Publication Data
Names: Peter, Wendy, author.
Title: Just getting started : stepping with courage into God's call for the next stage of life / Wendy Peter.
Description: Minneapolis, Minnesota : Chosen Books, [2021]
Identifiers: LCCN 2021023547 | ISBN 9780800762117 (trade paper) | ISBN 9780800762513 (casebound) | ISBN 9781493433520 (ebook)
Subjects: LCSH: Dreams—Religious aspects—Christianity. | Change (Psychology)—Religious aspects—Christianity.
Classification: LCC BR115.D74 P48 2021 | DDC 248—dc23
LC record available at https://lccn.loc.gov/2021023547

Cover design by Rob Williams, InsideOut Creative Arts, Inc.

Baker Publishing Group publications use paper produced from sustainable forestry practices and post-consumer waste whenever possible.

21 22 23 24 25 26 27   7 6 5 4 3 2 1

For Elizabeth,
who never stopped dreaming.

Contents

Foreword

Many are living frustrated and unfulfilled lives in this hour. Failed dreams, projects that have fallen short of initial expectations, and the feeling of being stuck in a rut with no forward momentum are not uncommon evaluations in the lives of many on the planet today. There are copious opportunities and resources available in these fast-moving days of modern technology and information, so why are many experiencing these discouragements?

Wendy Peter is a woman I deeply love and respect. She is a woman of character and integrity. She is one who selflessly champions others and is probably one of the greatest cheerleaders for others that I know. Wendy genuinely desires to see everyone fruitful, multiplying, fully satisfied and fulfilling their destiny in life. As you read *Just Getting Started*, you will feel as though you have your own personal mentor and coach. Her insights are motivating, inspirational and practical, and that is why many catapult into successfully fulfilling dreams and opportunities after sitting under her ministry.

Your best days are ahead of you. No matter what setbacks or discouraging situations you have experienced in the past, this is truly a new day for you to embrace. You were created to succeed. You were created to fulfill destiny.

One of my favorite examples of an individual committed to keeping his dream alive in the midst of much opposition and discouragement is Walt Disney. In his early days, he faced many discouragements. His first created character was stolen from him, and his next one was a mouse that no one was interested in. Many laughed at the very concept of using a mouse to capture the interests and affections of children. After all, mice are despised creatures. Why would anyone be interested in investing in a mouse as a star cartoon character? He faced one rejection after another as he submitted his dream to developers and investors, but his dream never faded. He believed in the mouse and its potential. Even after personal bankruptcy, his dream lived on.

Finally, his breakthrough day came and his persistence paid off. He found someone to see the potential of this mouse he named Mickey. The rest is history. The initial rejections and seeming failures were simply his starting point. Walt Disney passed away a number of years ago, but the mouse lives on. The creation of Mickey was only the beginning. He went on to create many more successful characters. One dream gave birth to many more. He created an entire experience for children of all ages called Disneyland, and another in Disney World. Multiple companies and franchises grew into global entities and are impacting the masses to this day. It all had a starting point that was marked by struggles and seeming failures.

If you are without vision for your life at this moment or you are struggling today with failed vision, feeling like you are stuck in a rut with no forward momentum, it is only the beginning. Your best days are ahead of you. You are just getting started! Don't be afraid to dream big—bigger than you have previously. Get excited as you watch God partner with you.

Foreword

This book is designed to encourage, build and establish you in your potential. Take your time as you read it. Meditate on its encouragements and teachings, and then activate. You will be amazed as you watch the life-transforming fruit materialize.

Patricia King, author, minister, television host

Acknowledgments

Thank you to Chosen Books and Baker Publishing Group for believing in me as an author. Thank you for the opportunity to share this message with people around the globe who want to launch their dreams but are not sure where to start.

David Sluka, meeting you was a divine encounter that changed the trajectory of my work as an author. Your kindness, patience and mentorship have had a deep impact on me in ways that I can never repay. You truly live your life as a "man for others" and demonstrate the teachings of Jesus in all that you do. I will be forever grateful for your influence in my life.

Patricia King, thank you for all of your wisdom, guidance, true friendship and love that you have poured into my life. You have inspired me to dream bigger, think higher and take steps of faith into the unknown again and again. I would not be where I am today without you.

Duane and Tamara Siemens, Russ and Brenda Alder and everyone at The Wave Church in Canada, thank you for your ongoing friendship, your support and your belief in me. You helped me build a foundation of godly character and Kingdom priorities within the local church. To every woman at The Wave Church who participated in my workshops when they were in the experimental stage, your willingness to dream big at any age was a part of the inspiration for this book. Thank you for sharing your lives with me and for trusting me to lead you during my time at The Wave.

To my team at Women on the Frontlines, this has been a challenging season, and you all have risen to the challenge of dreaming new dreams with me and stepping out to make a difference. Thank you for all the love and support you have given unconditionally to me as a friend and a leader.

My sister Elizabeth Thacker Atkins, you never stopped dreaming, even in the face of a terminal diagnosis. You traveled and celebrated, living life to its fullest during the time you had left. You were still making plans on the day of your departure. You reminded me throughout the writing of this book what really matters the most.

To my husband, Murray, and my children, Dayne, Blake, Grace, Mel and Jessica, you are my partners in dreaming and in living life to its fullest. Your ongoing support and love have given me wings to soar and eyes to see as I have launched into a whole new assignment during a time that has traditionally been seen as the retirement years. Thank you for who you are and all that you give me.

Introduction

In every one of our lives there are beautiful moments that seem frozen in time due to the deep and lasting impact they have on our hearts and minds. Much like a scene in a glass paperweight, we pick up the memory again and again. We look at it from every angle, revisit the moment and consider the ways that it has informed the person we have become.

Some years back after a season of personal failure and deep discouragement, I was at a very low point emotionally and spiritually. If you had asked me what my expectations for my future were, I would have replied, "What future?" Yet into that dark and empty scene in my life came a friend who had come back from her own time of failure but was now thriving.

When I told her of my inner emptiness, she replied, "Wendy, you just need to dream."

"I don't have any dreams left," I said.

She reached out, gently placed her hands on the sides of my face and stared deeply into my eyes. I could see in that moment that she had been where I was presently, and she understood the depth of my pain.

She whispered, "Wendy, I'll dream for you."

This book was birthed out of that beautiful moment, and it is my way of reaching out to you, wherever you are and wherever you have been, to say, "Don't give up. I'll dream for you."

"You are the salt of the earth, but if salt has lost its taste, how shall its saltiness be restored? It is no longer good for anything except to be thrown out and trampled under people's feet. You are the light of the world. A city set on a hill cannot be hidden. Nor do people light a lamp and put it under a basket, but on a stand, and it gives light to all in the house. In the same way, let your light shine before others, so that they may see your good works and give glory to your Father who is in heaven."

Matthew 5:13–16

1

From Hidden to Visible

You are the light of the world.

I was hidden until I was fifty.

That statement may conjure up images of baby Moses being hidden away in a basket by his mother or a secret room that hid a Jewish family during World War II. That is, of course, not what I mean. Rather, my potential was hidden, the realm of my influence was small, and the full force of my light was obscured to many, including myself.

> "You are the light of the world. A city set on a hill cannot be hidden. Nor do people light a lamp and put it under a basket, but on a stand, and it gives light to all in the house."
>
> Matthew 5:14–15

Jesus made a dramatic statement when He called you the light of the world and a city on a hill. He went on to say that our light and influence should not be hidden. It should be allowed to shine without hindrance so that our lives can have a life-changing impact on others.

Yet this did not match my reality as I turned fifty. I had carried big dreams and ideas inside of me for years and had made several attempts to step into the destiny that everyone in the Church seemed to be preaching about. I had done my best to serve my local congregation with a sincere heart and a strong work ethic, yet there was still a disconnect between some of the preaching that I heard and the reality of my actual experience. As I transitioned into my fifties, that disconnect was fast becoming a place of divine dissatisfaction within me, and I was not willing to keep my light under a basket any longer.

I had been asking a lot of hard questions about women, the Church and New Testament realities. One of those questions was, How is it that I have received so much good identity teaching and have been in many church services where God was moving, yet I still seem to be under such a false ceiling in terms of the dreams I carry? I was also asking myself why I was not experiencing the miraculous realm that Jesus spoke about to the degree that He promised His followers.

It seemed apparent to me that my reality was not living up to what was being preached, and it was becoming harder to reconcile the dreams that I carried within that reality. I had prayed for the sick for years and had seen some healed, but I wanted to experience more. The Bible was clear that Jesus had given His disciples (first the twelve, then the seventy and then all of His followers) the power to walk in a miraculous realm of authority where supernatural events happened on a regular basis. I longed to see that in greater expression in my life.

We can find this in the book of Luke in the Bible. "And he called the twelve together and gave them power and authority over all demons and to cure diseases, and he sent them out to proclaim the kingdom of God and to heal" (Luke 9:1–2).

And we can also see that Jesus called them to step into a greater realm of faith for daily provision than most of us would be comfortable with. "And he said to them, 'Take nothing for your journey, no staff, nor bag, nor bread, nor money; and do not have two tunics'" (Luke 9:3).

Jesus' disciples were dependent entirely on God, and they likely felt exposed and vulnerable. Their results, however, demonstrated that their light was shining with full force and was producing amazing results.

> The seventy-two returned with joy, saying, "Lord, even the demons are subject to us in your name!" And he said to them, "I saw Satan fall like lightning from heaven. Behold, I have given you authority to tread on serpents and scorpions, and over all the power of the enemy, and nothing shall hurt you."
>
> Luke 10:17–19

I had no idea at the time that in some aspects of my faith I was functioning more as a spectator than as a full-on participant in the Body of Christ. Like many around me, I was very involved in church. In fact, I was a leader in my church. To the outside observer, it may have appeared that I was fulfilling my calling as a Christian.

The reality was, however, that I had bigger dreams within me. My full potential was hidden at the same time that I was showing a dimmer version of it to others. I realize now that we can remain in the shallows of the call of God. We can keep ourselves busy with work that requires very little personal risk or faith while acting as a spectator of others who have waded deep with God into the realm of the miraculous, the realm of evangelism or any other realm beyond where most Christians are comfortable.

When you consider the contrast between your life and the following verse, what comes to mind? "And he said to them,

'Take nothing for your journey, no staff, nor bag, nor bread, nor money; and do not have two tunics'" (Luke 9:3).

A Life without Much Risk

Perhaps like me you find it hard to imagine setting out on a journey with absolutely no visible provision or plan. In our modern society it is easy to live a life where we are not required to risk much in the area of faith. We can remain largely dependent on our jobs, our doctors, our credit cards and our weekly church attendance as a substitute for risking it all.

Think for a moment about how the people around you would react if you decided to go on a journey to preach the Gospel and heal the sick, but you took nothing for your journey. What would they say? How would you respond to their reactions?

I am not suggesting that God requires that of us all, or that this book is about leaving home with nothing. I simply want to emphasize the contrast between the early disciples and us. Was their greater experience of authority and power connected to their greater willingness to risk everything to shine their light?

You see, my journey from hidden to fully visible required me to recognize that I had a very subtle root system of belief that was keeping me under a false ceiling (or a basket, to use the metaphor of our Scripture verse). This belief system hindered me from stepping into the fullness of my potential.

My mind was filled with vague ideas and uneasy questions such as, *Maybe I should not rock the boat too much. Maybe I am lacking the humility that I need. What if my desire to fulfill these big dreams is selfish ambition? Surely, going somewhere with no staff, bag, bread, money or extra shirt would be irresponsible, right?*

This kind of thinking was just enough to keep me where I was, somewhat hidden and somewhat unfulfilled, shining a bit of light but living below the radical impact that Jesus demonstrated in the gospels.

Divine Dissatisfaction

Divine dissatisfaction is a wonderful thing. It is an uncomfortable feeling in our spirit that helps us change, because we do not enjoy feeling that way. So if you, too, are feeling divinely dissatisfied in the difference between your current reality and your full potential, do not tamp those feelings back down. Allow God to stir them up as you read this book. He wants to call you up higher into a realm of greater effectiveness and satisfaction.

The season of divine dissatisfaction and frustration I experienced as I turned fifty was pulling me out of the shallows of where I had been and into a place of divine risk and excitement. I was heading toward a greater understanding of the unfettered glory and light that God wants to pour out of us and into the world. He wants to cause us to be such a contrast to the darkness around us that people can clearly see Jesus when they see us. For that to happen, we cannot stay hidden in the shallows of Christianity or keep our gifts and our light locked down. We need to take the risk to live out of our full potential, or we will not look much different from the world around us.

In our modern society it is easy to live in a place where we do not risk much in the area of faith.

"You are the light of the world" (Matthew 5:14). The Greek word for *light* used here in the gospel of Matthew is the word *phós*, which is defined by Strong's Concordance as "the manifestation of God's self-existent life; divine illumination to reveal and impart life, through Christ."[1]

According to this verse, we are called not only to shine and be visible to others, but we are to reveal and impart the pathway to life in Christ through the light we carry.

Jesus reenforced this idea in the book of John by saying, "I am the light of the world. Whoever follows me will not walk in darkness, but will have the light of life" (John 8:12).

He went on to heal a blind man shortly after making this statement, creating a physical demonstration of what it means to be a light and to open people's eyes to God. With His actions, He put on display His statement, "I am the light of the world."

God's expectation for all Christians is that we, too, are to be the light of the world just as Jesus is. We are to be fully visible rather than hidden, and people are to see us shine in our full potential. Through the above verse, He is telling us that our lives are to be lampposts that reveal divine illumination. All over the world, people are stumbling around in the dark and are confused as to what matters most, both now and in eternity. They need us to be the light that reveals His deep love to them.

That thought should be freeing to those of us who have remained hidden because of feelings of intimidation or worthlessness. While Jesus calls us the light of the world, it is not our assignment to manufacture the light. Rather, the Gospel at its core is that Jesus died so that we could receive His Spirit within us, and His Spirit is the light. Paul wrote about this when he said,

> For God, who said, "Let there be light in the darkness," has made us understand that it is the brightness of his glory that is seen in the face of Jesus Christ. But this precious treasure—this light and power that now shine within us—is held in a perishable container, that is, in our weak bodies. Everyone can see that the glorious power within must be from God and is not our own.
>
> 2 Corinthians 4:6–7 TLB

So when I am talking to you about stepping out of hiddenness and launching a new dream, I am not asking you to manufacture a new and amazing personality or to create supernatural outcomes through your own ability. I am inviting you to consider the fact that God wants to shine through you and color your confidence, your ideas, your choices and your future in new ways.

Like an individual piece of stained glass, you have a brilliance that is yet to be revealed. As you come out of hiding and let the full force of the light that is within you begin to shine without measure, you will color the world around you.

Where Did the Basket Come From?

When I look back at the early years of my upbringing, I can see some clues as to why I remained hidden as an adult. My family did not follow Christ beyond a cultural celebration of religious holidays, and because of this, Bible teachings on shining our light and living by faith were not shared with me. Also, the beliefs and messages that empower children to step past opposition and remain resilient in the face of rejection were missing. While my parents certainly loved their children, somewhere along the way in my family line certain relational tools had become lost or broken, and as such, they were not passed down. In fact, I experienced what some would describe as an old-school upbringing.

Receiving hugs, saying "I love you" and having calm discussions about our poor choices were pretty rare, and children were not asked for their opinions. Sharing your opinion as a child was called back talk in those days. In this environment, I was not encouraged to explore my own dreams, and any of my desires that were outside of the path of my parents (and their parents before them) were subtly discouraged. Those messages

I referred to earlier—stay hidden, do not rock the boat, maybe it is a lack of humility or selfish ambition to really put yourself out there—were rooted in the generational environment of my family. This may be true for you, too. The subtle messages that we all receive in our childhood can have the effect of dimming our light, our exuberance and our willingness to take risks, and it can be very hard to move past the beliefs and ideas that have been held for generations.

As I have taught dream-coaching workshops around the world and have asked people to identify the family messages that have kept them hidden or steered them to avoid taking risks, I have listened to people share many similar messages to those I heard in my childhood: Keep everyone happy; take the safe path or you will get hurt; avoid anything that puts the spotlight on you; do not travel too far or risk too much because that would be irresponsible; do not try to find a greater purpose beyond what we have shown you; no one in this family has ever _____ (fill in the blank with your dream).

Those early messages had an impact on me in ways I did not recognize at the time. As I became a young adult, I was not even aware that I was allowed to take a different path or to engage with a different belief system than what my parents had embraced. To use the words of Henry David Thoreau, we were, without realizing it, encouraged to "lead lives of quiet desperation."[2] We were to take our song to the grave and not place our light on a stand. We were, instead, to keep it hidden.

I recognize that there are those who want that hidden kind of life, but deep down I wanted more. So instead of inspiring me, my parents and their beliefs had limited me.

I know from talking to many people of my generation that this was not an unusual or extreme family experience. Some of the things that we experienced would be considered downright abusive in this day and age of helicopter parenting, therapy horses and "Do you want the red cup or the blue cup?" But my family's dynamic was typical of many homes of the era.

One result of this was that many from my generation found themselves following in the steps of their parents, while at the same time not knowing what to do with the dreams they carried that did not fit the accepted pattern of their family. So many of those dreams were put on a shelf or downgraded into acceptable forms of expression.

We did, however, give voice to those hidden dreams through the messages we conveyed to our children or to our nieces, nephews and Sunday school kids. We wanted them to experience a level of freedom and actualization that we felt unable to attain. So we raised them with deep wells of self-esteem, confidence and a litany of messages that communicated that they could do anything, be anyone or go anywhere they wanted.

And for a time as we were doing this, our nests were full, our bank accounts were stretched, our energy resources were maxed out and our schedules were bursting with dance classes, hockey practices and filling lunch boxes. It was both fulfilling and enough to simply tell our children to let their lights shine and to sing "hide it under a bushel—oh no!" while taking our turn in the Sunday school class. We could tell ourselves we had done our part in terms of raising the next generation.

It is and should be the work that we are most proud of. But for some of us, the day comes when the kids have grown up or moved out and we find ourselves sitting in the middle of our tidy nest that we have spent so many years feathering with Pinterest-worthy decor schemes. Our time is freed up, our resources are less limited, and we begin to long for the same sense of freedom and empowerment that we have communicated so enthusiastically to the children in our lives.

We assured them that they could do anything, be anything and go anywhere, but we failed to offer ourselves the same opportunities. In those moments as we look around at our well-built lives, we cannot help but ask, "What about me? Is this all there is for me?"

Perhaps those dreams you have carried for so long could be taken off the shelf and looked at again. Or perhaps you are re-examining your dreams through no choice of your own. You may have been impacted by a natural disaster, a global pandemic or another circumstance, and you find yourself looking for a new job or a new income stream as a result of events beyond your control. If that is the case, not only is this a moment in your life when change is at hand, but it is also an opportunity to come into greater alignment with a dream that will allow the light that God has placed within you to shine with greater force in your next season.

> *Like an individual piece of stained glass, you have a brilliance that is yet to be revealed.*

Whether you are in your twenties, forties, sixties or even your eighties, I hope that as we journey together through this book you realize you are never too young or too old to reinvent your life, step into a new dream or get started on a new project!

You are not alone in the journey, and the answer that you are looking for is not out there somewhere. It is contained in the light within you, and it is waiting to be uncovered in this season. Everything you need to step into your new dream is within you, because God is within you. And He has a plan for your next steps.

Unexpected Change

One of my favorite passages in the Bible is found in the book of Jeremiah. It was written to a group of people who had gone through a very difficult time. They found themselves exiled from Jerusalem, which was the home they had always known, and separated from the future they had expected to have. They were deported from their home country and carried off to a foreign nation where the customs were entirely different. This journey included having their houses burned to the ground and being forced to march to an unknown land with very few, if any, possessions or money. Life as they had known it for generations had evaporated before their eyes. I am sure that many of them struggled with feelings of hopelessness, uncertainty, loss and fear.

Certainly, some of them would have felt too old to be starting over. They had already built careers and homes, and many would have come to a point in their lives where they felt that their best years were behind them. Yet Jeremiah sent a message telling them to start over, even when it looked as though they had lost everything they had ever known. His message to them was to multiply and not decrease, to build houses, have children, plant gardens and start businesses. They were not to listen to the false prophets who would tell them it was all over.

"Thus says the LORD of hosts, the God of Israel, to all the exiles whom I have sent into exile from Jerusalem to Babylon: Build houses and live in them; plant gardens and eat their produce. Take wives and have sons and daughters; take wives for your sons, and give your daughters in marriage, that they may bear sons and daughters; multiply there, and do not decrease. But seek the welfare of the city where I have sent you into exile, and pray to the LORD on its behalf, for in its welfare you will find your welfare. For thus says the LORD of hosts, the God of Israel: Do not let your prophets and your diviners who are among you deceive you, and do not listen to the dreams that they dream, for it is a lie that they are prophesying to you in my name; I did not send them, declares the LORD."

Jeremiah 29:4–9

Jeremiah ends his message from God with these amazing words: "For I know the plans I have for you, declares the LORD, plans for welfare and not for evil, to give you a future and a hope" (v. 11).

Like the Israelites in this story, you may have recently gone through a time of crisis or loss. The Oxford dictionary defines *crisis* as a time when "important decisions must be made."[3] In the New Testament, the Greek word for *crisis* is the word κρίσις, and it is used several times to describe separating, selecting and making important judgments.[4]

The idea that a crisis is also a time of opportunity or a time to start over can be revolutionary. If everything in your life has been shaken and upturned, you may want to use these events as a time to sort through and decide what is worth giving your future effort to and what is not.

If this is what you are going through, I believe God's word of encouragement for you in this moment is the same message that He spoke to the Israelites through Jeremiah: "For I know the plans I have for you, declares the LORD, plans for welfare and not for evil, to give you a future and a hope."

The Stirring of Your Heart

You may have questions, and you may have fears about starting over or launching a new dream. You may feel that you are too old (or too young), that you have lost too much, or that you do not have the skills, education or background to match the dreams that God has placed in your heart. This is where I found myself as I was turning fifty. I had all of these questions swirling through my mind: *Why do I have these crazy dreams in the first place? Is my own ambition a divine call? Do I remain hidden, or do I need to press through into greater visibility and launch these dreams?*

I finally came to the conclusion that God was stirring these questions within me. He was calling me to step up and confront the false ceilings that I found myself under, and He was urging me to act as a trail blazer through an organization called Women on the Frontlines. He wanted me to call women out of their comfort zones and into greater places of influence where they could say with certainty, "This is what I was created to do."

And so, as we journey together though this book, it is my desire that you will find the answers to those important questions, as well as the inspiration and tools to shine your light as never before.

I want to end this chapter by telling you that it is not strange or weird that you have ideas, dreams and flashes of inspiration in which you see yourself in another life. It is also a good thing if you are unsatisfied by the gap between your daily reality as a Christian and the miraculous things you read about in the Bible. Those flashes, ideas and areas of dissatisfaction are the stirrings of your heart asking to be heard. My prayer for you is that those stirrings, which you may have been tamping down for years, will become too loud for you to ignore in the next few weeks and months.

> "You are the light of the world. A city set on a hill cannot be hidden. Nor do people light a lamp and put it under a basket, but on a stand, and it gives light to all in the house. In the same way, let your light shine before others, so that they may see your good works and give glory to your Father who is in heaven."
>
> Matthew 5:14–16

Questions for Journaling or Discussion

1. What are some ways you can see that your Christian experience does not have as great an impact on the world around you as the lives that Jesus and the first disciples lived in the gospels?

2. In Luke, Jesus sent out many disciples on a mission trip. He told them, "Take nothing for the journey—no staff, no bag, no bread, no money, no extra shirt" (see Luke 9:3). Why do you think He positioned them that way?

3. What are some of the subtle messages you have received throughout your life that taught you to hide your potential?

4. Do the people in your life encourage you to take risks, live out your dreams or expect the supernatural? If not, what is the message you are hearing from others around you?

5. What do you want to tell yourself after reading this chapter? In a few sentences, write yourself an encouraging note about your potential to shine your light and make an impact.

2

Your Destined Place

A city set on a hill . . .

Jesus not only called you the light of the world, but He also called you a city set on a hill (see Matthew 5:14). To understand what He is saying to us, we need to look at a bit of history. Depending on where you live, you may think of a city as a crowded, dirty or unsafe place. You may even dream of living in the country. But in biblical times, cities were the places to be. They were located in the hills so that they could be visible from far away and so that they would have a strong defense against any attack.

In the ancient world, cities were the hub of life and the center of commerce. Food, grain and oil were stored in safe places within the walls of the city to protect against times of famine and drought. Cities were also built around reliable sources of water that were inside the walls. It was designed this way so that there would be ongoing access to fresh water in the case of a long siege by an enemy. These walls were thick and fortified to keep out enemy invaders. So a city was where you would go if you were hungry, thirsty or in danger. It was a place that people who were in trouble went in order to have their basic needs met.

Jesus is saying in Matthew that you are not only called to be a light that shines to show people the way to God, but you are also called to be a visible source of provision and protection from the enemy. Like a city on a hill, you are called to be a person to whom others can turn in times of need.

If we look a little more closely at this verse, it also says something else very profound. It says that a city on a hill cannot be hidden. This means that when you are a place of provision, protection and healing, people cannot help but see you and be drawn to you. When you are lifted into the place of being a city on a hill, you will no longer be invisible!

This is an important point to understand. In my work in the ministry, I meet many people who are under a subtle deception that causes them to spend too much of their time trying to be seen, trying to attract followers or trying to be famous. Yet Jesus is saying that if you are in alignment with your gifting, you will not need to pursue fame to be visible. You will be like a city on a hill. You will generate a magnetic quality that will draw people to you. Passion is magnetic, authenticity is magnetic, generosity is magnetic, excellence is magnetic and miracles are always magnetic. We are drawn to these qualities. People will flock to you because they will be drawn to the light, love and provision that go with you when you are in full alignment with your dreams and purpose.

We can see this in the life of Jesus. Many times, He charged people to tell no one about His miracles (see Matthew 16:20; 17:9; Mark 7:36). But in spite of this, His fame spread everywhere. Jesus' brothers even tried to talk Him into going to Judea to make a name for Himself (see John 7:3–6), but Jesus refused to go to Judea publicly. Even though He intended to do the works of the Father privately, the results caused people to gather around Him.

Effectiveness Versus Fame

If we use the world's definition of success that declares bigger is better, we can think the call to dream is a call to become famous or build a huge enterprise. When we think that way, we can quickly disqualify ourselves because we believe we cannot attain that level of success. When the celebrity culture began to invade the Church, its effect was making everyday people feel as if they had nothing to offer that was significant compared to the famous Christians who were emerging. Things became unbalanced, and people began to follow and focus on leaders rather than Jesus. Too many leaders began to believe their own press and think they were extra-special people who should be treated with a superstar status. The atmosphere this created in the Body of Christ may have had an impact on you. It may have caused you to give up on your dreams because you felt as if you could not compete.

If that is you, I have some good news. Jesus is not calling you to fame—He is calling you to effectiveness. He is calling you to influence others right where you are using whatever you have in your hands. Most of His miracles were performed in everyday places with just a few people around; however, the impact of His actions has reverberated around the world.

Jesus was in alignment with God's highest purposes for His life, and this alignment caused Him to be both the light of the world that showed the way to the Father and a city on a hill—a magnetic place of provision, healing and protection that drew those who were in need. Pursuing fame and followers was not a part of the equation for Jesus, and it does not have to be part of the equation for us.

41

I watched an interview with Pastor T. D. Jakes in which he was asked to share one word he believed best described Jesus.[1] He shared the word *unhurried*. That word paints a clear image of Jesus walking with the Father in a relaxed state. He is not trying to accomplish something specific, but rather He trusts the Father that He will be a light to everyone He encounters.

In the same way, I believe that God is calling you to effectiveness rather than exposure. You do not have to hurry, nor do you have to fight for attention. God wants to simply lift you into greater alignment with your core gifts and abilities. He wants to put the *super* onto your *natural* so that you radiate passion, joy and excellence as you pursue meaningful goals. He wants to place you, like a city on a hill, into the most effective expression of your unique purpose and ability to make a difference in this next season of your life. The goal of this book is to help you come into alignment with the dreams God has for you. As that happens, you can trust that the right amount of visibility and influence will come in the right time.

> *Jesus is not calling you to fame—He is calling you to effectiveness.*

No More False Finish Lines

Now, before we go any further together, I want to check in with you on a couple of important questions. Is it possible that you may have stopped too soon in your pursuit of what God has for you? Is it possible that your vision for your life has been below that of being the light of the world or a city on a hill in the ways we have explored in these opening chapters? Let's consider that together.

Picture a running track that has a designated finish line. This finish line represents completing our assignments and fulfilling the potential that God has for us in our lifetime. Now picture a false finish line that is marked quite a bit before the real finish line. This finish line represents us prematurely stopping before we finish the race. Is there any chance that you have dropped out of the race too soon and stopped at a false finish line short of God's assignment for you?

The reason I want to address this issue early in our journey together is that too many Christians have disqualified themselves from the fullness of what God has for them. Like runners in a race who have dropped out long before the finish line, they have given up on that which God has stirred in them. They have lost their dreams somewhere along the way. They live in a place of knowing that there is more but being unsure of how to get to it.

The apostle Paul's words to the Galatians may speak to you if that is the case for you. He was writing to a group of people who started on a path of freedom and sharing the light of the Gospel with everyone around them. Somehow, however, they became sidelined, confused and focused on the wrong things. Paul said to them, "You were running a good race. Who cut in on you to keep you from obeying the truth? That kind of persuasion does not come from the one who calls you" (Galatians 5:7–8 NIV).

God does not want you to drop out early. I believe He wants you to complete the assignments and dreams He has placed within you, and that means you will need to recognize and reject any false finish line you have agreed to. These false finish lines can be any place where you have stopped moving forward because of things such as age, gender, opposition, finances, lack of resources and lack of opportunity.

We were created to dream, and as soon as we begin to dream something comes alive in us. Dreams make us fully alive because they bring us into partnership with the Dream Giver. You may never have considered it, but God needs a vessel for His dreams. You are that vessel. He would like to partner with you to live out His dreams through your realm of influence. Without the partnership of human beings, God is limited as to how He can move in the earth.

So you and your dreams are much more important to God than you may have realized. He needs you to be both the light of the world that reveals Him and a city on a hill to the lost and needy. And all God needs is your yes to move you away from disqualifying yourself and move you into the realm of permission. Permission to dream is the pathway to possibility thinking, and that is the place into which I want to invite you to activate your dreams.

Possibility Thinking

What is possibility thinking? Is it a slogan for public speakers? No, it is much more than that. When you give yourself permission to dream, you are stepping onto a pathway where you can consider your future with fresh eyes. It is as if you can see a new finish line off in the distance instead of the false finish line where you stopped previously. You have a new perspective and a fresh hope. You see possibilities and potential where before you only saw problems and roadblocks. You see an opportunity for a second chance.

In the past, you may have seen yourself as ineffective or without much to offer, but I want to call you to lift your eyes up and consider what it would mean if you were just getting started. What would it mean if the things that have sidelined you in the past were no longer issues to you? What could the possibilities be if you were just getting started in your dreams?

As I travel across the nations hosting my dreams seminar called Let Your Dreams Take Flight, I always open the seminar by pointing out that if you are going to launch a new dream, you will need to consider some higher possibilities for your life. You will need to open yourself up to imagine living a life that is totally different from where you have been and what you have done before. In essence, you will need to change the expectation you have had for your future.

If you are currently living on government assistance, for example, and your dream is to run your own business, then you will need to be able to imagine not being dependent on the government for finances. You will need to see yourself stepping up higher, opening a business and maybe managing a store and employees. Can you see it? That place of higher vision that you are seeing is a picture of you when you have stepped into your potential and are shining with authenticity and influence like a city on a hill.

If your dream is to lose weight, you will need to start by considering that it is possible for you to do so rather than believing that you are unable to change and will always be overweight. You must be able to consider your life as different from what it is now, seeing yourself fit and healthy and doing things that perhaps you have been unable to do because of being overweight. You will need to allow God to lift you into a new mindset to see yourself in the place you have longed to be: a light to the world, a city on a hill.

Resurrecting the Seed of Your Dream

If the part of you that was created to dream is shut down, it may be hard for you to imagine your life as any different from what it is. Or perhaps you are realizing that you used to have dreams, but they are dormant and sitting on a shelf like the runner in the race who had been sidelined.

Well, I have good news for you. We serve a God of resurrection who loves to resurrect that which was dead. The seed of your dream may be old and it may be lying on the shelf, but everything that it needs to flourish is still in the seed of that dream. No matter how old your dream is, it can be taken off the shelf and brought to pass with the right attention and condition for growth.

Even in the natural realm this is true. Theories on the absolute maximum lifespan of seeds were shattered when a Japanese botanist uncovered lotus seeds in a layer of peat at the bottom of a dry lakebed in Manchuria that were thousands of years old.[2] When a germination test was carried out, nearly all of the lotus seeds sprouted. Scientists were astonished. The peat in the lake was thought to date back to the Ice Age.

Another incredible resurrection of old seeds came in 2005 when the extinct Judean date palm was brought back to life after some of its 1,900-year-old seeds that had been recovered at the ancient fortress of Masada (AD 73) were revived with a water bath and a dose of fertilizer and hormones.[3]

The date palm Methuselah emerged from the soil, bringing the species back from extinction. It has now gone on to multiply and produce offspring trees. That is right, Methuselah went from dead and extinct to fruitful and abundant. All it took to reactivate those old seeds was changing the environment they were in.

Think about that for a moment. A seed full of potential sat for thousands of years and did nothing. Then, when exposed to the right conditions, the seed activated, grew, flourished and reproduced. This is true of our dreams as well. Those sparks of vision in which you have seen yourself in a different life are the seeds of your dreams. They may have been dormant for years, but just like the date palm in the story, they can grow when they receive exposure to the right environment (which I hope to provide throughout this book). Your dreams can not only become active, but they can grow, flourish and reproduce.

You were created to dream and become the full expression and demonstration of everything you were meant to be. You were not created to be sidelined or placed on a shelf. God did not put the seed of potential into you only to leave it inactive. Max Lucado said, "You aren't an accident. . . . You weren't mass-produced. You aren't an assembly-line product. You were deliberately planned, specifically gifted, and lovingly positioned on earth by the Master Crafts-Man."[4]

As you work through this book, God is going to do three things.

1. He is going to change the way you think.
Breaking free from the limitations that you and others have placed in your life will allow you to consider new possibilities and opportunities that have never occurred to you before.

2. He is going to resurrect some old dreams.
Revisiting your old dreams, soaking them in the water of God's Spirit and fertilizing them with your faith is going to create the right conditions for them to spring back to life.

3. He is going to conceive some new dreams in you.
You may only have lived out your parents' dreams, or maybe you have not dreamed at all. God is going to give you a new and fresh dream in this season that activates your purpose and makes you want to jump out of bed in the morning to take on your day with new zeal.

> *If you are going to establish a dream, you must first dream the dream.*

Activation

So let's get you dreaming with an activation that I do in my Dreams Take Flight workshops.

We all have what I call a "limiter" in our mind. This limiter has a list of objections and perceived barriers that act as a false ceiling or box that we cannot seem to get past. In order to tap into God's dream for your life. You will need to be intentional about moving past that limiter.

First, find a comfortable place to sit. Put on some quiet instrumental music that you feel will help you relax and open up your mind and imagination. The Bible says, "Now glory be to God, who by his mighty power at work within us is able to do far more than we would ever dare to ask or even dream of—infinitely beyond our highest prayers, desires, thoughts, or hopes" (Ephesians 3:20 TLB).

This activation will be the most important exercise that you will do in this book, because it will trigger a moment of lift for you. What is a moment of lift? It is a moment when our perspective changes and we receive a higher vision for our life. Lies and limitations are shattered, and possibilities and new perspectives come into play. Picture God lifting you up out of your present circumstances and limitations and placing you into alignment with your ordained destiny in Him. He can place you as a city on a hill where you are no longer striving to try to make a difference; instead, you are releasing what is in you, and it is making the impact you have always longed to make.

I did this activation under God's direction while alone in my basement some years ago, and it changed my perspective in major ways and led me to the place of effectiveness and influence I am in today. So I want to invite you to experience the same kind of encounter that I had.

Activation Instructions

1. Find a quiet place where there are no outside distractions. Get a pen and paper, or perhaps a journal if that is what you use normally, to record your thoughts.

2. Put on some quiet instrumental soaking music that you find conducive to relaxation and that helps you to connect with God.

3. Now, close your eyes and think about the following question for several minutes:

   If there were no barriers of any kind, if money was not an issue, if time was not an issue, if opportunity was not an issue, and if I knew for sure that I would succeed . . . what would my amazing life look like?

   Stay with your visualization for several minutes and ask God to open up the possibilities. Ask Him to reveal your unfulfilled dreams to you. Allow Him to move you past the limiter in your mind.

4. What kind of picture do you see? Where are you? What are you doing? Who is with you? Write out a description of what you see, even if it is just in the form of bullet points right now.

In the years that I have been running Dreams Take Flight workshops, I have never worked with a person who did not see a higher vision for his or her life than what he or she was living out currently. Without exception, each person I have worked with in my seminars has experienced a *moment of lift*. Their dream may have lacked definition, but it was there. They could see the seed of their dream. Their vision had shifted.

Your moment of lift is not simply a glimpse of a fantasy. Your dream is much like the ungerminated seed we talked about earlier in this chapter. It exists in seed form with everything hidden inside of it that is necessary for its maturity, but it has not yet been exposed to the right conditions to cause it to thrive. The goal of this book is to create those conditions for you and get you past the limitations that are holding back your dream. Whether those limitations are mindsets or practical realities, they act (in the words of Matthew 5:15) as baskets that obscure your dream and dim the full force of your light from having an impact on the world. Over the course of this book, we will work on removing them one at a time and changing your environment. There is a right environment for your dream to prosper in, and it is possible to create it and see results.

Now, let's finish this chapter by beginning to identify the limitations that are holding back your dream. I find it is best to do this while the dream is still fresh in your mind. Let's do a final activation.

Now that you have pictured what your life would look like if there were no limitations, what would you need to find or overcome to step into the dream you have pictured? Circle the ones that apply and make any notes that come to mind about what you think you need.

Definition: the dream lacks clarity
Resources: tools, equipment, manpower and finances

Opportunity: open doors, favor and influence

Time/Timing: life is too busy, or I have believed it was too late or too soon for my dream

Fear of failure or a lack of confidence: help to believe in myself and my ability to carry it out

According to the Bible, *you* are the light of the world, and *you* are a city on a hill that cannot be hidden. The Bible was not written only to that famous Christian teacher you may follow on Facebook or admire from a distance. You are needed, and your gifts and abilities matter to God. He wants to partner with you to successfully launch the dreams He placed into you before you were even born. Now is the perfect time for you to get started!

3

Moments of Lift

. . . cannot be hidden.

*B*ut, Patricia, I don't want to be famous."

It was November 2017, and I was sitting in a small Italian restaurant with my friend and mentor, Patricia King.

She had just asked me to become the director of Women on the Frontlines in Canada. Her invitation for me to step into a greater realm of influence had come because of the potential that she had seen in me as we had worked together the previous several months. I was experiencing a moment of lift—or rather I was resisting it, considering the words that had come out of my mouth. But either way, I had been on a long journey of faith that had led me to this moment when my dreams were being taken off the shelf. I was receiving an invitation for them to be fulfilled.

A moment of lift when you receive a higher vision for your life or when you experience a new open door for your dream may feel as if it happens quite suddenly, but there is usually a journey of preparation that precedes it. God has called us to be a city set on a hill, and one way He accomplishes this is by bringing moments of lift into our lives. His purpose during these seasons is to position us into alignment with the place where we can be released into our dreams.

Most of us have been taught culturally that through our own plans and strength we can do anything we want, and to some degree that is true. But this book is not just a list of directions on how to imagine, organize and pursue a dream in your own strength. I want to invite you to come into alignment and partnership with God's personal dream for you, and I want to help you discover your *why* that makes you want to get up in the morning to pursue that dream in order to make the world a better place.

Your *why* is different from your *what*. Your *what* is the thing you do (the dream), but your *why* is the force behind it (the reason). It holds the passion that makes what you do magnetic to others. Your *why* is unique to you and is developed through your life journey and lessons. I want to share some of my story that preceded my moment of lift that occurred with Patricia in the Italian restaurant. In doing so, I hope that you will see the similar ways that God has used your journey to develop your *why* and to prepare you for your own moments of lift that will bring you into divine alignment with your dream.

That journey for me started in 1983 at a Christian camp. At the young age of nineteen years old, I had been sent to sort myself out. I needed to get away from some of the unsavory characters I had been involved with prior to my conversion to Christianity. My days at the camp were spent standing at a sink washing hundreds of dishes, and my free time was spent alone in my room or walking the shores along the lake.

While this may not sound like a moment of lift to you, it was for me. I had been lifted out of a life where I had been living with criminals who broke into people's homes, sold drugs, lived to party and had no ambition to do anything different. I escaped from this situation in the middle of the night with just the clothes on my back after placing a desperate call to some sweet Christian ladies who had shown interest in my well-being.

From the time I met those ladies, I had been in a transition. Drawn magnetically toward their light, their difference, their peace and their joy, I began to find my lifestyle empty and unsatisfying, and I was longing for whatever it was that they seemed to carry within themselves. One night after some deep soul searching and realizing that I was trapped in a life with some very dangerous people, I found the courage to dial the phone number that one of the women had left me in case I ever wanted to leave.

They bundled me off to an old-fashioned Mennonite Christian camp. They realized that the type of people I was involved with would not take kindly to their interference in my life, so the camp they chose was located far away from where I had been living. I went from a glamorous but broken party girl dressed in heels and sequins to standing in front of a massive sink of dirty dishes with an old white apron tied around my waist, my hair back in a ponytail and no makeup on my face.

In retrospect, I know that this was a moment of lift and an alignment that God had arranged so that He could place His dream within me. I was unable, however, to see this at the time, and I was having trouble relating to the new environment in which I had been placed. As I stared at the endless mound of dirty dishes placed before me each day, I felt like a fish out of water.

These moments of lift in which God calls you higher can be very uncomfortable. The upgrade into a new role or experience can place you with people who are functioning at a different level spiritually, financially, with their level of influence or in regard to their character. As you look back, perhaps you can recognize situations when, at the beginning of the transition, you did not really fit.

This was the case for me at the Christian camp. All of the ladies wore long calico skirts and blouses. They looked to me as if they had stepped out of the *Little House on the Prairie* television series. They had left a set of these clothes out for me in my room, but I refused to wear such a strange—at least, to me—outfit. I can only imagine what they must have thought of me as a new convert coming out of such a wild lifestyle. I must have seemed as odd to them as they seemed to me.

The wife of the older camp leader came to talk to me. She told me that it was important that I wear the long skirts and blouses that they had provided for me as it was a part of their culture. I took great offense at her request and stormed out of my room. I decided at that moment that I would run away from the camp. As a new convert, I had very little understanding of how spending my days washing dishes and going to chapel services could lead to a better life. I was quickly becoming disillusioned with this new path I had chosen. And I certainly was not going to dress up like Laura Ingalls Wilder just to make them happy!

So with my few possessions bundled into my backpack and no plan other than to try to hitchhike somewhere new, I trudged the five miles from the camp to the main highway. I spent that walk wondering how I had gotten myself into such a strange situation. At that moment, my party lifestyle and criminal friends appeared in my mind as much better than they really were, and I regretted having called the church ladies.

The Way Up Is Down

Well, God had other plans for me. The camp was located in a fairly remote location, and after I stood beside the road for hours, only one car came along and slowed down to offer me a ride. The driver was the old German cook from the camp. After inviting me to get in, he simply turned around and drove me straight back to the camp! God was apparently determined that we were going to do things His way and not mine. It is humorous now to look back at this inauspicious start to my dream, but at the time, it seemed anything but funny.

In retrospect, however, I am grateful that God turned me around and took me back to that camp. The experience of "lift" into an upgrade in your circumstance, anointing, character or role requires change. If you do not take the lesson God has provided to help you come up higher, you will end up going around the proverbial tree over and over until you pass the test and acquire what God is trying to give you. That day as the car headed back to the camp, God was taking me right back to the lesson He had planned for me.

Later that day as I cried alone in my room, I had my first genuine encounter with the tangible presence and call of God. I knew nothing of the Bible, so I simply opened it to a random page.

It opened to the book of Titus, and these words were magnified to me:

> Older women likewise are to be reverent in behavior, not slanderers or slaves to much wine. They are to teach what is good, and so train the young women to love their husbands and children, to be self-controlled, pure, working at home, kind, and submissive to their own husbands, that the word of God may not be reviled.
>
> Titus 2:3–5

As I read these words, the presence of God enveloped me. I saw myself as an older woman standing before a crowd of thousands of women, speaking to them. I heard the voice of God whisper to my heart, *I am calling you into the ministry. You will teach and encourage women around the world. But right now, I want you to learn from the women I have placed over you. Now wear the dress and wash the dishes!*

A moment of lift is a moment in which our perspective changes, we receive a higher vision for our life. Lies and limitations are shattered, and possibilities and new perspectives come into play.

And so it began. God, who is the Alpha and Omega, had shown me the future. He had called me to preach and teach His Word, and His plan for this dream started with me in a long calico dress, standing at a sink of dirty dishes and learning the basics of Christianity—humility and obedience.

You Have Been Preparing Your Whole Life

This place of partnership and alignment with God's dream for you will often include a journey that seems to have many twists and turns. These might be hard to understand at the time, but, in retrospect, they can be seen as an essential part of what God is preparing you for. That is why it is important to never disqualify yourself as too old for your dream. The reality is that you have likely been training and preparing for this season your whole life. Like Esther, you may have been called "to the kingdom for such a time as this" (Esther 4:14) to appear suddenly on the stage of humanity so that you can have an impact on many. It is very possible that you have been preparing your whole life for this exact moment in time without even realizing it.

Such is the story of Chesley Sullenberger, who is known affectionately as Captain Sully. He was an unlikely hero who landed an Airbus A320 on the Hudson River in New York after a bird strike crippled the jetliner's engines two and a half minutes into the flight. In an interview after the incident, Sullenberger said that he realized he was too low to return to LaGuardia or to make an emergency landing at Teterboro. "I knew immediately that this, unlike every other flight I'd had for 42 years, was probably not going to end with the airplane undamaged on a runway."[1] Even recognizing that, Sullenberger said, "I was sure I could do it." He continued, "In many ways, as it turned out, my entire life up to that moment has been a preparation to handle that particular moment."

This is also true for you. God may have you on a journey that looks rather like a maze with a variety of twists and turns. These twists may at times seem to lead nowhere and cause you to feel sidetracked from your dream. But these turns are not without a purpose in what He has been preparing you for. You might not have given them much thought before, but even the disappointments and the rejections that you have experienced inform your sense of justice and compassion. They, too, can be a part of what God has laid as a foundation for your next season.

Forming Your *Why*

After the season I spent at the camp, I experienced many other moments of lift. Some were positive, such as meeting a wonderful Christian man who was full of integrity and joy and who asked me to marry him. This moment of lift planted my feet fully into the soil of God's Kingdom by giving me a companion who was faithful and committed and who believed in me more than I believed in myself. Other moments of lift were not as wonderful or as easy to understand in terms of the ways that they were preparing me for what was to come. As I look back, however, I can see the many ways they informed and created the *why* behind the passion I now carry for Women on the Frontlines.

One time I heard an announcement that there was going to be a training meeting for anyone who felt called into full-time ministry. I was beyond excited, and I spent weeks writing out and preparing my vision statement. When I arrived at the meeting, however, I was told that the leader had assumed everyone had understood that he was only looking for men. I found this rejection to be quite devastating. In reality, however, there were very few leadership roles available to women at the time. I added *equality for women* to my *why*, and I continued on my journey toward my dream.

Then there was the time that I approached the leader of the new church we were attending and announced that I would like to be the women's minister. I felt that with my call to full-time ministry this would be an easy fit. I imagined planning large, beautiful events for women with fancy centerpieces and gourmet food. I was told, however, that they already had a women's leader. I was welcome, though, to take on a role no one wanted, which was leading an inner healing class for women.

I had no experience in this, but I agreed to do it, naively thinking, How hard could it be? I found myself with a group of very nervous women who were sitting in a back room with a book I was supposed to lead them through called *The Door of Hope*.[2] Talk about the blind leading the blind. I am pretty sure I was the most emotionally shut down person in the whole group. But in spite of that, the seed of the dream God had planted in me kept me moving forward. As I attempted to help those ladies recover from their emotional wounds, I found myself being healed along the way. Once again, a moment of lift was occurring in my life even though it did not look like what I expected. I subconsciously added *the journey from brokenness to wholeness* to my *why* and continued to simply work in the local church in whatever ways were open to me.

The closed doors, rejections or experiences that seem as if they are sidetracks are usually either deep lessons in character development or specific aspects of anointing that God wants to equip you with for your future assignments. Like a beautiful vessel that a potter is creating at his wheel, the vessel will seem to be nearing completion only to have the potter bring it back down to the base again. Like the potter, God is removing hidden flaws and refining you. This happens each time His hand moves you or holds you back.

This theme of God inspiring my dreams while at the same time resisting my attempts at fame or influence continued for many, many years. I received prophetic words from visiting prophets who talked about me being called to the nations and being surrounded by a multitude of spiritual children, even while there seemed to be no correlation to that in my everyday life. While I watched others around me take off into their international callings, it appeared that I was to remain hidden away in a little church in Canada. In the end I learned to simply do whatever was in front of me to make the world a better place for those with whom I was in contact. My dream to travel the world as a teacher and minister seemed totally out of reach, and I had come to a point where it no longer mattered to me.

You see, I had found my *why* as I worked in the local church over the years. I had come to love people for themselves, and I found no greater joy than supporting them in their journey from brokenness to beauty and from bondage to freedom. By this time, I had become a very proficient communicator and teacher of the Bible, and I was writing curriculums, teaching small groups and filming videos. I was even able to preach on Sundays from the pulpit after being ordained and licensed as a minister. And the fact that this had happened in a city where there were very few licensed and ordained women had been a significant moment of lift for me.

I was unaware that, like Captain Sully, everything that had happened up to this time had been preparation for what God was getting me ready to do. Every dead end, every rejection and every stopping place had been forming my *why* and my character. Every obstacle and injustice I had fought to move past had strengthened my core faith, and my years of hiddenness had burned out my need for fame and recognition.

So I was really quite happy and content at the beginning of 2015 when the subtle feeling of divine dissatisfaction came upon me that I described in the first chapter. I had no idea why I was stirred up so suddenly, but I could not shake the feeling that a shift was about to take place.

I hope you will be very encouraged by what happened next in my story. You may be reading this book and saying to yourself, "There is no apparent evidence that anything extraordinary could happen to me that will bring my dream to fruition." You must remember, however, that we serve a God who moves in the realm of *suddenly*, and a sudden change was about to come into my life.

Spiritual Acceleration and Divine Alignment

At this point, I did not know Patricia King. I had only seen her at a distance when I attended the first Women on the Frontlines conference held in Canada in 2012. I distinctly remember sitting in the very back row of the conference and being moved in my heart by all that Patricia was carrying for women. I did not, however, meet her personally, and I had no connection with the Women on the Frontlines ministry that she was leading through conferences and events around the globe. So it was only by the Holy Spirit's prompting four years later that I clicked on a Facebook post written by Patricia that one of my friends had shared.

As I read her words and saw her face, I heard these words in my spirit: *Go to Arizona.*

What? Arizona? Why would I do that? I put the thought immediately out of my mind. Arizona was far from Canada and expensive to travel to in 2015. So I brushed it off. I had no real connection to Patricia or any reason to get on a plane to go visit her. Yet the Holy Spirit continued to drop this thought into my heart.

Go to Arizona. I would hear it throughout the day. It was there when I woke up each morning, and it was there when I was trying to fall asleep.

Go to Arizona. Go to Arizona. It was honestly one of the most illogical experiences I had ever had, but I could not shake it, and it would not go away.

I finally responded and chose a weekend mentoring event that Patricia was hosting in Maricopa, Arizona. I booked myself a flight and a hotel. I will never forget how foolish I felt sitting in my seat on the airplane heading somewhere for no reason, except for the fact that a persistent message kept leaping through my spirit. To combat the voice of logic that was telling me that I was crazy, I kept quoting to myself, "The just shall live by faith" (Romans 1:17 NKJV).

Have you ever been stirred in your spirit to step out in faith and do something you have not done before or that makes no sense in the natural? This may be God getting you ready for another moment of lift that will lead to a season of spiritual acceleration to propel you into your destiny.

The women's event in Arizona was very good, although I was well-versed in the topics that were covered. So I realized that I was not there for only the conference. With this in mind, I tried to keep my spirit open and sensitive. I listened to the gentle prompting of the Holy Spirit's voice as I interacted with the people whom I met over the course of the three days. And while I made a couple of friends, I did not meet Patricia personally, except during a question-and-answer time at the end of a session.

During this time set aside for questions, I stood to ask a question of Patricia. After answering me, she paused and said, "I see something on you that is really special, and God is going to use you in a big way." Her words did not, however, point to anything specific.

I came home with a handout for a new group Patricia was launching called Women in Ministry Network. I felt drawn to the group. Thinking that perhaps this was why God had wanted me to fly to Arizona, I joined the network. And then I went back to the life I had been living in Canada and in the little church in Winnipeg.

One year later, Patricia was hosting a global Women on the Frontlines event in Phoenix, Arizona. The prompting of the Holy Spirit started up again. *Go to Arizona. Go to Arizona.* I still had no idea why God wanted me to go. This time, however, as soon as I started to receive the inner direction, I knew I would follow it. Then, to save a bit of money, I posted a request for a roommate in the Women in Ministry Network Facebook group that I had joined after my first visit to Arizona. Incredibly, this one simple step began a series of events that led directly to where I am today. And it demonstrates so clearly the way that God is often working behind the scenes in our lives.

A young woman replied to my request to share a room, and we met up at the airport the day we landed in Arizona. I did not know anything about her, but over the next several days of the conference we shared our hearts deeply and became great friends. Now, here is where the super comes onto the natural. My roommate's name was Brandi Belt. It turned out she was a young woman who Patricia was training to be the next-generation leader for Women on the Frontlines. When she agreed to room with me, she did not know that Patricia had already booked and paid for a room for her elsewhere in the hotel. As she had already committed to share a room with me, she honored her commitment, and we spent the weekend together.

That weekend we spent as roommates became a hinge that swung open the door to the next season of my life. What was remarkable was that I was just being myself as I shared my heart, my passions and my friendship with Brandi. Yet within three months of that conference, I was invited to host a Women on the Frontlines event in my hometown. Then, within a year of the conference, I was sitting across from Patricia in the little Italian restaurant with her asking me to lead Women on the Frontlines in Canada. The current leader, Faytene Grasseschi, was stepping away from her role to pursue her dream of influencing the realm of politics. Patricia was looking for a woman who had the potential to fill her role.

This moment of lift, from hidden to visible and from dreams on the shelf to dreams in full play, came to pass because God put His super on the natural when I stepped out in faith and obedience to follow His voice to Arizona. He then released another moment of lift and supernatural alignment when I followed His prompting to reach out for a roommate.

This place of divine alignment included sharing a room with Brandi, who was not even supposed to be in a shared room but somehow was. It also included Brandi carrying the same passion I carried for empowering women and the fact that she was connected to Patricia King. This also happened at the same moment that Patricia was looking for someone to step into a role with Women on the Frontlines. That is a lot of unlikely things coming together, but it is truthfully what happened in my story.

And I believe God wants you to be encouraged—it can happen in your story, too. God wants to align you with your dream and your season. Sometimes it means radical obedience to the prompting of the Holy Spirit, and sometimes it involves supernatural alignment of things that are beyond your control. But I believe that if you do your part, God will do His part. Then, as you respond to His leading, you will see a time of spiritual acceleration and divine alignment come into play.

Do It for Jesus

Now back to my conversation with Patricia King at the little Italian restaurant. She had just asked me to step into the role of director for Women on the Frontlines Canada and explained to me that the role would mean extensive travel and a very public profile as an influencer.

Even though this should have been a very exciting moment for me, because the dreams that God had planted in me years ago were now coming to fruition, the first words that came out of my mouth in response to her invitation were, "I don't want to be famous."

I went on to explain to her that I knew that this level of exposure and influence would be like having a target painted on me, and people would feel free to critique my every word and action. I also knew that strangers would contact me and make demands of me. I think I might have even thrown in the word *stalkers* to my list of reasons for being hesitant to step up to the role. I told Patricia that over the years, my desire for fame, fortune and influence had been burned out of me by my long season of being hidden. I was happy as I was, being ordained and serving as an associate pastor in a local church, preaching occasionally on Sundays and running small women's groups in the church basement.

I was not in ministry for money. That was not my *why*. I was not in ministry for fame. That was not my *why*. My *why* had been refined to the simple act of taking women from places of brokenness to wholeness. My *why* had become about helping every woman I was in contact with feel seen rather than invisible. It was about helping them feel a part of something bigger than themselves. My *why* was about helping people develop character and deep connection with Jesus. It was not about getting any personal attention.

Patricia could not only see my *why* shining through in everything I did, but she could also see the potential for me to lead an organization like Women on the Frontlines precisely because I was not infatuated with fame and fortune. She knew that the *why* inside of me and the grace I had as a speaker and teacher had much greater potential to have an impact on women than I was currently walking in.

So after listening to my list of all of the negative things that come along with a very public role, she said, "Wendy, I know you don't want to be famous, but would you do it for Jesus?"

She had me at "Do it for Jesus."

And so, in November of 2017, I said yes to a new role and a new season. At 52 years old, I was stepping into a new ministry and, in the words of the title of this book, I was just getting started.

The years of hiddenness had taken me from the *what* of my dream, which I had seen clearly 35 years before at the church camp, to refining the *why* of my mission.

Now that you have heard my story, let's think about yours. In the activation that you completed in chapter 2, I asked you to sit quietly and invite God to reveal an image of what your life could look like if money, time, opportunity and confidence were not an issue. During that meditation, you likely had a glimpse of your dream and of being lifted into a higher level of impact. You likely saw your *what*—just as I saw mine as a young woman at the church camp when God impressed my heart with the image of me standing before thousands of women. That was my *what*, but not my *why*. My *why* was revealed through my years of testing and life experience.

I know that your journey and life experience have developed a sense of *why* within your dream as well. So in the next chapter, we will look at your dream and help you to define clearly not only what you want to do, but also give voice to the *why behind it*.

I believe that as we work together through this, you will find the kind of dream within you that is so compelling and completing to your life that you want it at all costs. A dream that makes you willing to take any test and make any adjustment necessary to experience the lift you need to achieve it.

Questions for Journaling or Discussion

1. When you think back over your life, have you ever found yourself in a situation that did not make sense or did not line up with the dreams you carry? List a few of those experiences that seemed to lead nowhere.

2. What have you learned from those times? Can you identify any moments of lift into a higher place of character or anointing that came from those times?

3. Jot down three to five of your most powerful memories from your life. These memories can be positive or negative.

4. What are some of the strong desires and beliefs that you took away from those experiences? These desires and beliefs are what begin to form our *why*.

5. Do you see any messages from those memories that have had an impact on your desire to help others or make the world a better place?

4

Defining Your Dream

You are the salt of the earth.

*H*ave you ever thought about how totally unique each human being is? With our one-of-a-kind combination of looks, personality, giftings and abilities, God did not make us bland, boring or the same. He gave us each a unique flavor to express through our lives, and I believe that He wants our distinctive flavor to color everything we do.

We have been looking at the book of Matthew in the Bible. In the passage we are studying, Jesus not only told us that we were to be a light and a city on a hill, but He also called us salt. Salt is an ingredient that is absolutely necessary to our life and health. Our bodies need it to stay in balance. It has a distinctive taste, and it brings out the flavor of anything to which it is added. It is often used as a preservative, and it was so valuable in Jesus' time that it was often used in trade and currency. And interestingly, given our topic, some ancient people put salt on the wicks of lamps to increase their brightness.[1]

When you apply this metaphor to yourself, you can see that Jesus is saying that you are absolutely necessary to the life and health of the Body of Christ. Like salt, you are distinctive in your flavor. When you come into contact with others, your distinctive flavor will enhance and bring out the flavors of those you influence. You are here to help preserve and protect the purity of God's will and Word in the earth, and as you do this, you will increase the brightness of the light of those you influence.

Jesus went on to say, however, that if salt loses its flavor, it becomes useless. It gets thrown out and trampled underfoot, and it loses its intended purpose.

> "You are the salt of the earth, but if salt has lost its taste, how shall its saltiness be restored? It is no longer good for anything except to be thrown out and trampled under people's feet."
>
> Matthew 5:13

Scientifically, it is impossible for salt to lose its flavor as it is a very stable chemical compound. In Jesus' time, salt would sometimes be mixed with other ingredients but still sold as pure salt in the marketplace. When it was discovered that the salt had lost its flavor, it would be thrown out into the street.[2]

I love this part of the metaphor that Jesus used. It speaks to an important truth that I have seen again and again as I have hosted Dreams Take Flight seminars: It is impossible for you to lose your original flavor and your distinctive design. God has placed a unique DNA and set of gifts inside of you that function as the salt that Jesus calls you to be. Your DNA and gifts enhance everything about you and around you when they are activated.

The problem is that you may never have taken the time to tap into those unique gifts and callings. You may never have established what matters most to you, because you were too busy serving other things. Your salt may have gotten lost in the mix. We each have a special and unique flavor. If we lose that, we can lose our sense of purpose and destiny.

When I work with people to help them launch their dreams, I like to take them though the process of defining their dream in detail. This is the equivalent of isolating their unique flavor and expression and drawing it forth from the mix of their life. This involves not only defining what they want to do, but also defining the *why* that fuels their dream. So I want to invite you into this same process as you work though this chapter.

In chapter 2, I asked you to picture what your life would look like if money, time, opportunity and clarity of purpose were not an issue. Think for a moment about what you saw in that picture. What where you doing, and why were you doing it? You may be able to answer these questions clearly, or the answers may be fuzzy and unclear. Do not worry if it is still fuzzy. We will come back to this statement at the end of the chapter, and by then it should be much clearer to you.

I want to (what do you dream of doing?)

because (why do you want to do it?)

Examples:

- **I want to** stop the trafficking of children, **because** it is sinful.
- **I want to** start a jewelry business, **because** I want to create beautiful things that minister to women.
- **I want to** become a national worship leader, **because** I want to influence people to follow Jesus.
- **I want to** help women lose weight and regain their health, **because** the devil is stealing their destiny with obesity and sickness.

- **I want to** sell good-quality used cars to people, **because** they deserve an honest experience, and this will be a witness of God's Kingdom.
- **I want** to go to Paris, France, **because** it is a bucket list dream that will make me happy.

You will notice that there are a variety of dreams on this list of examples. There are business dreams, ministry dreams, health dreams and travel dreams. There is no right or wrong dream. In fact, there may be several dreams stirring in your spirit right now.

I would like you, though, to identify one specific dream to work on as you go though this book, one that you believe flows from your unique sense of purpose and calling in God's Kingdom. Simply put, ask God to help you identify what specific dream you should work on in this season. Once you learn to flex your dream muscle and get this dream off the ground, you will find it is easier to step into the other dreams that God has for you to complete over your lifetime.

God has placed a unique DNA and set of gifts inside of you that function as the salt that Jesus calls us to be. Your DNA and gifts enhance everything about you and around you when they are activated.

Defining Your Dream

Let's get started defining your dream. It may have been easy for you to fill out the *what* and *because* statements above, or it may still feel fuzzy to you. You may have seen the *what* when you did the activation in the first chapter but still have trouble identifying the *why* behind it. Both are important. Along your path to success, you will have difficult days that are filled with challenges and mistakes. On those days, you will find that a well-defined dream that includes a strong sense of *why* will help you stay strong.

I believe that, as simple as it sounds to define your dream, many do not take this important step. As a result, they are kept from fulfilling their destiny. Instead of taking the time to lay out the *what* and the *why* that are in their heart, their dream remains a vague fantasy. Is your dream vague or fuzzy? A vague dream will be hard to explain to others and hard to hold on to when tests and challenges come. I think it is fair to say that Jesus does not want your dream to remain only a vague and fuzzy idea, because He said that in a bland state in which we have lost our saltiness, we will get thrown out and trampled underfoot.

I have met a lot of people who feel as though they have been thrown out and trampled underfoot by life. They usually have a trail of disappointing experiences behind them. Yet when I explore the problem with them, I can see that their dreams have never gotten off of the ground due to a lack of a clearly defined vision. It is as if they have not taken ownership of their particular flavor and focus, and they have not established what really matters to them.

Too often they have found themselves serving someone else's vision in which they do not fully believe. When this occurs, they come to a point where they are not even sure why they are still in the room with the person they are following. I hear from these people that they have lost their sense of purpose and feel cast aside much as Jesus described in this passage in Matthew.

If that is you, I want you to know that it does not have to be this way. I have seen again and again that once people take ownership of their passion and define clearly their unique and personal dream, their dream gains momentum. As this happens and you establish a higher vision for your life, it will be easy for you to let go of that which is lesser.

Part One: Identifying Your *What*

Let's start by clearly identifying what you want to do. Over the years, you may have taken a personality test or a spiritual gift test—or perhaps this is all new to you. Either way, I believe that by working through the exercises in this chapter, you will be able not only to isolate your potential, but also to to unlock some creative ideas to give your dream a specific focus. Even if you have taken some of these surveys in the past, it is a good idea to do them again and ask yourself the question, Is this still true for me? As we evolve and grow, new desires can emerge and hidden gifts can come to the surface. By looking at your life with fresh eyes, you may unlock a new desire or dream that is ready to be launched in this season.

Jesus has called you light and salt and said that you are to be visible and a refuge, like a city on a hill, for others. This points to having a specific focus (or sphere) of influence that flows toward others out of your unique passion and personality. So let's look first at seven different spheres of influence to help you identify which ones you are already involved in, or perhaps want to be involved in, as a part of your dream.

The Seven Spheres of Influence

In 2013 Lance Wallnau and Bill Johnson released a book called *Invading Babylon.* In the press description of the book, the writer said:

> Before church was established as a place that people "came to," Jesus instituted it as an army that brought transformation to society, starting with salvation and continuing with seven

spheres of influence: Church, family, education, government, media, arts, and commerce.[3]

Identifying which spheres of influence you are connected to or are passionate about can help you define your dream.

To which of the following seven spheres of influence are you connected? If you are not connected to any, which ones cause you to be stirred up with a desire to have an impact or influence on them? Circle the top two or three that stir you.

religion	education	government
family	media	arts/entertainment
	business/commerce	

Ministry Gifts

Now let's look at your ministry gifts. Did you know that the Bible tells us that we have each been given specific ministry gifts by the grace of God? Which of the following ministry gifts do you function in that also give you joy and satisfaction? Choose your top two.

> We have different gifts, according to the grace given to each of us. If your gift is prophesying, then prophesy in accordance with your faith; if it is serving, then serve; if it is teaching, then teach; if it is to encourage, then give encouragement; if it is giving, then give generously; if it is to lead, do it diligently; if it is to show mercy, do it cheerfully.
>
> Romans 12:6–8 NIV

Preaching/prophecy (spiritual needs): Declares the will of God and keeps people centered spiritually.

Serving (practical needs): Renders practical service to help others.

Teaching (intellectual needs): Instructs, corrects and does research to keep others learning and growing.

Encouraging (identity needs): Draws others to see the vision, the possibilities and the good. Keeps others moving forward.

Giving/contributing (material needs): Renders material aid to others as a representative of Christ.

Leading/administrating (functional needs): Provides organization and direction in order to improve function and to apply vision.

Compassion/mercy (emotional needs): Provides emotional and personal support and love.

When you look at this list, I hope that you can see that everyone has a part to play in God's Kingdom. Being able to recognize your particular spiritual bent will be a part of planning out your dream. Two people, for instance, may be called to the family sphere of influence. If one of the people is gifted with superintending and administration, they will usually think in terms of organizing a team of people to minister to families, or to perhaps launch a business that meets the needs of families. The other person, who is gifted in the area of compassion, however, will often be happier working one-on-one or dealing directly with people—perhaps being a counselor or running a vacation Bible school for kids.

This is why it is so important to take ownership of your unique identity and celebrate who you are. As I said before, we each have a special and unique flavor. If we lose that, we lose ourselves. The Bible uses the analogy of the parts of a body to say that each gifting is as important as the others.

For the body does not consist of one member but of many. If the foot should say, "Because I am not a hand, I do not belong to the body," that would not make it any less a part of the body. And if the ear should say, "Because I am not an eye, I do not belong to the body," that would not make it any less a part of the body. If the whole body were an eye, where would be the sense of hearing? If the whole body were an ear, where would be the sense of smell? But as it is, God arranged the members in the body, each one of them, as he chose. If all were a single member, where would the body be? As it is, there are many parts, yet one body.

1 Corinthians 12:14–20

Hobbies and Areas of Interest

Now let's add one more survey to look at when defining your dream.

For too long, Christians have misunderstood the call to live a godly life as being a call to separate themselves from everyone and everything in the culture around us. Unfortunately, we have, by default, kept ourselves out of many of the mountains of influence within society. I do not believe that this was ever Jesus' plan for His people.

I believe that God is calling Christians to represent Jesus every day using their normal lives, hobbies and interests to build a realm of influence in the culture. We are to be salt, light and a city on a hill to our neighbors and friends. For too long we have tried to reach the lost only through hoping that they will decide to come to our church. The problem is that many people in our culture do not want to come to church at all. The answer to this dilemma is to simply bring church to them. Oh, and by the way, you are the Church, and where you go, Jesus goes, too.

Let's look at your hobbies and areas of interest to see if there are one or two in which you excel. These simple hobbies and interests can be an opportunity to partner with God in His dream to reach all of humanity with His love and salvation. The Bible talks about this in the book of Ephesians. "So be careful how you live. Don't live like fools, but like those who are wise. Make the most of every opportunity in these evil days. Don't act thoughtlessly, but understand what the Lord wants you to do" (Ephesians 5:15–17 NLT).

Are there any unique skills, hobbies, interests or passions you carry that could be directed into an area of influence? Some of these areas overlap, but these categories should help you pinpoint a few.

Practical skills—working with your hands: woodworking, cooking, gardening, sewing, automotive repairs, photography or any other practical skill.

Physical skills—working with your body: sports, recreation, camping, hiking, traveling or any other physical skill.

Intellectual skills—working with your mind: skills you can teach others such as finances, technology, theology, gaming or any other intellectual skill.

Health and wellness skills—working with mind, body and spirit connection: nutrition or health coaching, emotional healing.

Other skills: Anything unique that you can do that can be shared with others.

Your Seedbed of Dreams

You may have disqualified yourself from the dream that God has placed in you because you have imagined that those who are used greatly by God are extra special. You may have seen a particularly fruitful individual who you admire, but compared to them, you have felt as if your life does not measure up. If you have not seen that kind of fruit in your life, you may have believed that you do not have a valid dream.

Yet God does not give us the finished product. He gives us a seed. What you have admired as extra special in others is most often a mature dream that started as a single seed. When you see fruitfulness, you are looking at the season of mature growth and harvest in someone's life. But all of that fruit came from a seed. It was planted, and it grew into its potential.

Similarly, God has placed the potential for your dream within you in seed form. It is there in the character traits, interests and personality that you carry. All of the characteristics you have identified in this chapter's surveys are actually seeds that can grow into the dream that God has for you. He is inviting you to scan your life for seeds of potential.

Do you find yourself drawn to solve problems for everyday situations? You likely have the seed of administration in you. Do you love to explain to your friends how simple it is to complete a task that you are good at? You have the seed of teaching in you. Every accomplished teacher who you admire from a distance started with a seed of teaching. What seeds do you see in your life? When you can identify those seeds and ponder how they can be used to have an impact on the world and build God's Kingdom, you have moved into possibility thinking.

Part One Activation

Write down the combination of areas of influence, ministry gifts, and one or two unique hobbies or interests that you have circled. These will become the "seedbed" of your future dreams. Here are a few examples:

Susan
Spheres of influence: family, media

Ministry gifts: teaching, compassion

Hobbies, interests, practical skills: crafting for her home

When Susan connects the dots, she is inspired to start a social media coaching show to help stay-at-home moms in their parenting. She demonstrates simple crafts and activities they can do with their children to make learning fun, and she engages in online discussions to answer their questions.

Bill

Spheres of influence: business, government

Ministry gifts: administrating, encouraging

Hobbies, interests, practical skills: public speaking, financial coaching

When Bill connects the dots, he recognizes that he has always had a dream to help change his city. He decides to run for office as a city councilor on the platform of financial integrity.

John

Spheres of influence: education, family

Ministry gifts: teaching, encouraging

Hobbies, interests, practical skills: hockey, fishing, car repair

When John connects the dots, he is inspired to launch his dream of coaching young men into maturity. He starts a drop-in program using his areas of interest and skills as a magnet to draw young men. He teaches them auto repair and runs a casual hockey team that meets once a week. John coaches and encourages the guys naturally as they hang out together.

Now list *your* spheres of influence, *your* spiritual gifts and *your* practical skills and hobbies here:

Spheres of influence:

Spiritual gifts:

Hobbies, interests, practical skills:

When you look at it all together, what possibilities have you stirred up?

business dream	ministry dream	family dream
justice dream	creative dream	travel dream
fun dream	community dream	any other dream

What can you imagine? Write down key words and phrases.

Part Two: Finding Your *Why*

Now let's talk about finding your *why*. When you begin to think about answering the question "What is my *why* that fuels my dream?" you will want to look at what really matters to you or brings you joy when you work at it. As a motivating force, there is a big difference between acting from duty and acting from passion. Duty springs from "I have to," while passion springs from "I get to." When you are working out of your passion, you will feel excited before you start, and you will feel satisfied after you finish—no matter how difficult the thing is that you are tackling. In contrast, when you are serving out of habit or duty, you will often feel pressured and unmotivated before you begin and resentful after you finish.

Finding your *why* is especially important if you are stepping into a role that has been created for or held by someone before you. If you do not understand your own *why*, you may end up serving the vision of the person before you and never find your own vision. You will also have people who served the former leader choose to leave, and if you have not found your own vision for the role you are in, you may internalize their lack of support as a failure on your part.

But when you define your dream fully, including your *why*, you will recognize clearly the fresh, relevant assignment that God has given you for right now. So whether you are starting out on a totally new path or have had the honor of receiving a ministry, business or opportunity that was birthed by someone else, you should clearly define your dream. Doing so will give you the clarity to take full ownership of the new season in which you find yourself.

Our *why* is found in the realm of our emotions and motivations, and it is the force behind our dream and the passion that keeps fueling it. When you add your *why* to your dream, you are stating the reason that your dream matters. One of my dreams is to stop the trafficking of women and children. When I think about my *why* behind this dream, I feel strong emotions that include anger that this is happening, compassion for the women and children, excitement at the potential of rescuing people and a strong desire to stop human trafficking because it is wrong and sinful. I know why it matters to me.

If I was defining this dream, I would say: "I want to stop the trafficking of children because it is wrong and sinful, and I want to make a difference."

Your *why* will be unique to you. I have heard many over the years.

- Because this issue I am tackling is wrong/sinful.
- Because I want to make a difference.

- Because I want to make my parents proud.
- Because I want to change the culture.
- Because people deserve _____ (fill in the blank).
- Because it will give me joy.
- Because I am moved with compassion.
- Because I want to raise up the next generation.

If you discover that your *why* is only because you want to be rich or famous, you may want to look deeper into your dream and find some stronger reasons to pursue it. Fame and money are never satisfying in the long term, and if they are your only reasons for pursuing your dream, you will lose your fuel when money is tight or when you find yourself doing hard work behind the scenes with no one noticing. You will need a deeper reason to keep going and a more compelling sense of why. Oftentimes that reason is born in an experience that moves your emotions strongly in connection to your dream.

I remember Patricia King saying to me, "Wendy, you will need to get down to the heart of your mission with women." I had been working on my dream in an intellectual sense by writing down my reasons for ministering to women, but my *why* went much deeper when I was marked by God's Spirit as I was ministering in Lethbridge, Canada.

It was Mother's Day weekend, and minutes before I was to preach, God stirred up some difficult memories around my relationship with my mother and how I had felt as if I could not please her when I was growing up. I was not sure what was going on with those memories, but after discussing it with Patricia, I decided to share my pain openly with the women I was ministering to that night. As I shared my story with the women, I began to hear a deep sobbing break out in the audience. Women were weeping because they, too, had struggled with abandonment, rejection, feeling invisible or feeling as if they did not measure up with their mothers.

As we ministered to those women at the altar, I was marked in the Spirit with my *why*. I was moved deeply to see them going from brokenness to wholeness, and I felt totally satisfied in my spirit to be partnering with God in their healing. I have since had other moments of being marked with my *why* behind my ministry, and they have almost always come through a strong emotional response and a recognition of the satisfaction of doing God's will in the earth.

Jesus had this same sense of satisfaction after ministering to a woman at a well who had a history of brokenness and loss (see John 4:7–26). After introducing Himself to this woman as the Living Water and taking her on a journey from lost to found, Jesus turned to His disciples and said, "'I have food to eat that you do not know about.' So the disciples said to one another, 'Has anyone brought him something to eat?' Jesus said to them, 'My food is to do the will of him who sent me and to accomplish his work'" (John 4:32–34). Jesus knew His *why* for His time on the earth, and He was living from a place of divine satisfaction as He fulfilled it.

Part Two Activation

As we turn to work on defining your dream again, let's add in your *why*. I would encourage you to sit with this and allow God to narrow your focus. If you have several possibilities of dreams in your mind, then take time to pray and ask God to reveal to you which dream you should work on in this season. Try to write it out in a couple of simple statements. We will work on expanding it later, but for now, let's define it as simply as possible.

I have included the examples from the beginning of the chapter for you to look at for comparison.

I want to (what do you dream of doing?)

because (why do you want to do it?)

Let's look back at some of the examples I shared at the start of the chapter.

- **I want to** stop the trafficking of children, **because** it is sinful.
- **I want to** start a jewelry business, **because** I want to create beautiful things that minister to women.
- **I want to** become a national worship leader, **because** I want to influence people to follow Jesus.
- **I want to** help women lose weight and regain their health, **because** the devil is stealing their destiny with obesity and sickness.
- **I want to** sell good-quality used cars to people, **because** they deserve an honest experience, and this will be a witness of God's Kingdom.
- **I want to** go to Paris, France, **because** it is a bucket list dream that will make me happy.

You should have narrowed down your dream into a fairly simple starting place. If you have done that, then you have identified your seed. You are ready to plant it, water it and watch it spring to life like never before.

The Heart of the Matter

As you have worked through the surveys in this chapter, you may have thought, "I have done this before, and it hasn't gotten me anywhere." That may be true, because you can take personality tests and ability assessments all day, and they will only remain information unless you get down to the heart of the matter.

What is the heart of the matter? I believe that question centers around who God wants to be in your life in this season. I believe that He wants to be the Alpha and Omega to you, the one who knows the beginning from the end, and the one who created you and placed His divine purpose within you at the start of your life. He is not finished with you, and I also believe that you are not finished yet.

In fact, if you look around the world and the state it is in, you will see quickly that your dream is needed desperately to help save this world from the direction it is heading. God is looking for solution makers at this exact moment in history. The world might have run out of solutions, but God has not. Your unique combination of personality, gifts and abilities can bring fresh solutions that no one else may have. You can reach people no one else can reach, because God has uniquely designed you to reach them.

Now is not the time to allow the past or the circumstance you are in to hold you back. Now is the time to activate your faith and believe that the Alpha and Omega who created you, gifted you and planted the seed of a dream inside of you is going to take you into the fulfillment of that dream!

5

Staging Your Comeback

Nor do people light a lamp and
put it under a basket . . .

Courage.

You need it to fulfill your dream.

The dictionary defines *courage* as "the ability to do something that frightens you,"[1] and I know from my own experience that one of the greatest barriers you will face while bringing your dream to completion is fear. You might be facing the fear of failure, the fear that you have not really heard from God, the fear that you are too old, too young or ill equipped for the dream, or any number of other fears. Whatever the fear is that is stopping you, you will need to access courage to move past it if you are going to succeed.

My favorite definition of courage came from my friend David Braun during a sermon he was preaching at our church camp in Canada. His definition shifted my mindset and released me to receive courage as never before. He said simply, "Courage is when the pressure on the inside is greater than the pressure on the outside."[2]

When I heard this definition, I pictured dreams pushing up on the inside of people. This image should help you remember that whenever you lack the courage you need for your dream, you can allow the positive pressure of God's dream for you and His promises to you to break you out from under anything that is holding you back.

The psalmist said, "I sought the LORD, and he answered me and delivered me from all my fears" (Psalm 34:4). God did not create you and give you His gifts, abilities and potential only to have you keep them hidden. The Scripture we have been studying says it this way: "Nor do people light a lamp and put it under a basket" (Matthew 5:15). Fear will keep you hiding your light, but courage will break you free. God can deliver you from every single fear that is holding you back from your dream.

It is time for you to make your comeback and step into your destiny. God did not fill you with His light only to have you hide under a basket. It is time as never before for you to get out from under what has been holding you back and dimming your light.

So let's look together at some of the most common fears that can hold back your dream. As we do this, I want you to invite God to release His courage within you. You can break free from each one of the fears that you have until the basket that you have been under is sitting in pieces at your feet, never to be a hindrance again. That is His promise to you. And as we look at each one of these baskets, I will give you practical activation steps to help you release your courage and break free.

The Basket of Age

Every fear is based on a lie. A very common lie that holds people back from their dream is that they feel too old or that they are running out of time. Let's talk about being too old for your dream. The Bible is full of stories of heroes of the faith who experienced their greatest moments of purpose and influence during their last season of life.

One of these heroes is Moses, who was used powerfully by God to deliver the children of Israel from slavery. His entire life was a preparation for the moment when he would confront Pharaoh and lead the children of Israel out of Egypt. "Now Moses was eighty years old, and Aaron eighty-three years old, when they spoke to Pharaoh" (Exodus 7:7).

Moses' preparation for this moment included forty years of working for his father-in-law, Jethro, as a shepherd in the desert spending his time in ways that would appear unrelated to his dream to help his people. Those forty years reflect a time frame that we might think of as the best years of his life, a time when a person would have the most energy and fire to accomplish his or her dream. Yet when Moses encountered God and was commissioned to go to Egypt, God was silent on the issue of age. In fact, when Moses said to God, "Who am I that I should go to Pharaoh?" God said simply, "I will certainly be with you" (Exodus 3:11–12 NKJV).

I believe that this is God's word to you, too, if you are launching your dream at an older age. God is with you. He will strengthen and empower you as you wait upon Him and are filled with His Spirit in this season.

In saying this, I do not want to minimize the physical journey we take in our bodies. As we get older, we do not have the same physical strength we had in our twenties. While it may be true that you have less physical stamina, you have much more wisdom, experience and anointing to bring with you into your dream. And the Bible promises that God will renew your strength so that you can complete the assignment He has for you. In Isaiah, God spoke this promise to Israel, and I believe it is His promise for you, too.

Have you not known? Have you not heard? The LORD is the everlasting God, the Creator of the ends of the earth. He does not faint or grow weary; his understanding is unsearchable. He gives power to the faint, and to him who has no might he increases strength. Even youths shall faint and be weary, and young men shall fall exhausted; but they who wait for the LORD shall renew their strength; they shall mount up with wings like eagles; they shall run and not be weary; they shall walk and not faint.

Isaiah 40:28–31

You may be in your seventies carrying a dream that you received many years ago, like my friend Rae. Rae was 72 when she attended a dream workshop I was teaching. She told the class her dream centered around performing Christian comedy. Unbeknown to her, Rae's dream was about to come to fruition.

Here is what happened. As a part of the class, all of the participants were asked to create presentations about their dream to share with the others. When Rae's turn came to present, she had written an entire comedy routine that was really funny. She had all of us laughing, and we could see her light shining through with her special gift of humor. Following her time in class, the door swung open for her to fulfill her dream. She received requests to do her comedy presentations in homes for seniors. Rae told me it was fulfilling to see that she could have an impact on others by being unafraid to step into her dream—even as a senior.

Another friend, Donna Krueger, lost her husband suddenly. After an initial season of loss and confusion, she decided to sell her home, buy a recreational vehicle and go on a road trip adventure, which had always been a dream. Donna had many profound and hilarious experiences as she traveled in her RV.

She chronicled these experiences in a book called *Driving with the Light*.[3]

She had never written a book before, but she told me, "I waited so many years to fulfill these dreams. I thought, 'Why not? What do I have to lose?'" So at age 77, Donna published her first book. This, in turn, opened doors for Donna to become a sought-after speaker at women's events.

The idea that your age will hold you back from fulfilling your dream is just that—an idea. And it is a belief that is being left in the dust as forty becomes the new thirty, fifty the new forty, and people around the world are giving themselves permission to reinvent their lives at any age.

In fact, a Twitter thread went viral when television writer and producer Melissa Hunter tweeted, "At the end of 2020, instead of 30 Under 30 and NextGen lists, please profile middle-aged people who just got their big breaks."[4] Older men and women from around the globe began to tweet their incredible stories of starting over, reinventing their lives and launching their new dreams in their fifties, sixties and seventies.

How old is too old? Do not ask Tom Moore about being too old. Or I should say Sir Tom Moore? At one hundred years old, he was still setting goals and living out his dreams.[5] Moore raised an astounding 33 million pounds for health care workers during a global pandemic after setting a goal to walk one hundred laps around his garden leading up to his one hundredth birthday. His story lifted the spirits of so many people in the United Kingdom that Queen Elizabeth knighted him and changed his name to Sir Tom Moore.

There are many more stories I could tell, but the reality is simply this: If you allow age to be a basket that dims your light and holds back your dreams, it will. But if you will decide as Rae, Donna and Tom did to step up and step out into your dreams, that basket will disappear and will no longer hold you back.

The Basket of Identity

As you can see from looking at the basket of age, the way you view yourself can have a profound impact on your ability to start over and launch a dream. Your past, your culture, your gender and your place in society can also try to speak to you as reasons to hold you back. In order to successfully launch the powerful vision God has placed in your heart, it is important that you confront any limiting beliefs that you have attached to your identity.

Over the years, I have noticed that following any upgrade or increase in my assignment or realm of influence I have always had my identity tested. As God releases into you His picture of who you are called to be, that picture will always clash with whatever you believe that is below His viewpoint. Like Moses, your initial thought when you receive a dream from God might be, "Who am I to go and do this thing God has asked of me?" And just like Moses, you will need to receive the truth that no matter what your past, your gender, your cultural background or your place in society, if God has given you the dream, then certainly He is with you.

Jesus also had to pass the test of owning the identity and purpose God had given Him. In Luke, Jesus was baptized by John in the River Jordan, and God spoke a powerful identity message over Him. "You are my beloved Son; with you I am well pleased" (Luke 3:22).

This message was a public confirmation not only of Jesus' identity, but also of His mission. It had been prophesied for hundreds of years that God would send the Messiah, a Son who would save Israel from their sins.

Yet immediately following this moment of lift and confirmation of His identity and purpose, the Bible says that Jesus was led into the wilderness by the Spirit to be tested by the devil. We can see in the book of Luke that two of His tests began with a challenge to His identity: "If You are the Son of God . . ." The other test tempted Jesus to live below His purpose by worshiping the devil and dimming His true light through the false opportunity of fame and fortune in this world rather than receiving His true identity and purpose as the Messiah and resurrected King:

> And Jesus, full of the Holy Spirit, returned from the Jordan and was led by the Spirit in the wilderness for forty days, being tempted by the devil. And he ate nothing during those days. And when they were ended, he was hungry. The devil said to him, "If you are the Son of God, command this stone to become bread." And Jesus answered him, "It is written, 'Man shall not live by bread alone.'" And the devil took him up and showed him all the kingdoms of the world in a moment of time, and said to him, "To you I will give all this authority and their glory, for it has been delivered to me, and I give it to whom I will. If you, then, will worship me, it will all be yours." And Jesus answered him, "It is written, 'You shall worship the Lord your God, and him only shall you serve.'" And he took him to Jerusalem and set him on the pinnacle of the temple and said to him, "If you are the Son of God, throw yourself down from here, for it is written, 'He will command his angels concerning you, to guard you,' and 'On their hands they will bear you up, lest you strike your foot against a stone.'" And Jesus answered him, "It is said, 'You shall not put the Lord your God to the test.'" And when the devil had ended every temptation, he departed from him until an opportune time.
>
> Luke 4:1–13

It is important that we understand the purpose of what was happening in this story. The word used for *test* in this portion of Scripture is the Greek word *peirazó*, which is translated "to

95

make proof of."[6] And what I want you to see is that as soon as you receive and define your God-given dream, the devil will attack your identity and purpose.

Yet God has a redemptive purpose in the test, which is to *make proof of* and solidify your identity and purpose as it relates to your dream. As this happens, you will go through spiritual battles where your past, culture, circumstance, gender, age and experience will seem to be magnified as the reasons you cannot fulfill your dream.

Yet God is in the test with you, just as He was with Jesus. The Bible said that Jesus, who was full of the Holy Spirit, was led by the Spirit into the wilderness to be tested. The pressure on the inside of Jesus (the Holy Spirit) was bigger than the pressure on the outside (the attack against His identity and purpose).

This is also true for you. When God gives you His dream, the light and purpose of that dream on the inside of you is bigger than the pressure of anything on the outside. It is bigger than your past, your culture, your gender, your finances or anything else that you believe will hold you back. And the purpose of this testing is to *make proof of* your dream, just as it was for Jesus.

You can see in this passage that Jesus defeated the devil's sly accusation that He was not the Son of God not by defending Himself, but by upholding and declaring God's words as having the highest authority. This included the Father's declaration of His identity and purpose. "This is my beloved Son, with whom I am well pleased" (Matthew 3:17). Jesus had to win an internal battle of aligning Himself with the Father's words above everything else. He took ownership of His identity by submitting to and upholding everything that God had spoken of as right and true. He was locked onto what God said, and that had greater weight than anything the devil had to say about it.

Take Ownership of Your Identity

The way out from under the basket of a negative identity is not only to come into alignment with what God says about your dream, but it is to take ownership of your upgraded identity and see yourself the way God sees you in the dream. Let His word be the final word about you and your dream until what He says is your reality. You need to let the positive pressure of God's dream within you rise up and overpower the negative pressure and limitations that are outside of you.

If you want others to see you as the CEO of a company or the head of a ministry, for example, then you must see yourself that way. You need to accept God's call and assignment and believe fully that what He has promised will come to pass. And most important of all, you must bring an end to the process of defending your identity. Come down off of your mountain of testing and get on with what God has asked you to do!

This is an important key that I am sharing with you. In my years of coaching women and men who are pursuing their dreams, I have met too many people who have spent years taking one inner healing course after another. Instead of letting these courses help them regain their confidence, they have lost it. They focused for so long on their brokenness that they never felt healed enough to launch their dreams.

While I believe inner healing can be an important part of your journey, what I want you to see is that Jesus did not remain endlessly on the mount of temptation trying to defend His identity. He came down off of the mountain of testing in the power of the Spirit that was inside of Him. He headed back to His hometown and made a courageous announcement about His mission right in the midst of those who had little faith in who He was.

The story is found in the book of Luke:

And Jesus returned in the power of the Spirit to Galilee, and a report about him went out through all the surrounding country. And he taught in their synagogues, being glorified by all. And he came to Nazareth, where he had been brought up. And as was his custom, he went to the synagogue on the Sabbath day, and he stood up to read. And the scroll of the prophet Isaiah was given to him. He unrolled the scroll and found the place where it was written, "The Spirit of the Lord is upon me, because he has anointed me to proclaim good news to the poor. He has sent me to proclaim liberty to the captives and recovering of sight to the blind, to set at liberty those who are oppressed, to proclaim the year of the Lord's favor."

Luke 4:14–19

If we were to continue to read Luke's gospel, we would find out that those who did not believe in Jesus rose up against Him. They made accusations against His identity and purpose such as, "Isn't this the carpenter's son?" They even tried to throw Him off the edge of a cliff. But Jesus had already been tested at the edge of a cliff in the wilderness and had passed that test. The power on the inside of Jesus was greater than anything they could throw His way at their cliff. The Bible says simply, "But passing through their midst, he went away" (Luke 4:30).

Now, that is an amazing story about Jesus. He went into the wilderness, passed His identity tests, made a bold announcement about His mission and scattered His enemies.

How do you apply this to yourself and your mission? If you are not going to continue to take inner healing classes, how can you get locked into a firm place in your identity as Jesus was? I would like to give you three keys that are woven throughout this Bible story that I have practiced and often teach on my coaching weekends. I have seen these keys bear fruit in my life and in the lives of others.

Three Keys to Breaking Free

1. Deal purposefully with the weak spots.

While I do not agree with taking endless inner healing classes, I do believe that it is a good idea for you to pray about your dream and ask God to show you any limiting beliefs that you carry about life or yourself that will trip you up later in the journey. Make one or two appointments to pray through these issues with a trusted friend or a counselor to remove any wounding at their source. The Holy Spirit led Jesus into the wilderness where He had an opportunity to settle any limiting beliefs. This process of identifying limiting beliefs and receiving healing for the root issues is a normal step in realizing your dream.

2. Establish an internal hierarchy of authority.

Once you have identified any limiting beliefs or identity messages and have forgiven those who caused them, you will find that it is time to walk out and exercise your upgraded identity. You can do this by creating what I call an internal hierarchy of authority. What do I mean by this? I mean that you need to decide intentionally who has the right and authority to speak into your identity and purpose. Who has the right to speak into your dream? Ask yourself, "To whom do I want to give the authority to speak into my dream?"

Your identity, your dream and your future should not be open to everyone's opinion. Jesus exercised His internal hierarchy by placing what God had to say about Him at the top and what the devil had to say on the bottom. He limited the devil's authority to tell Him who He was or to speak to His purpose. He limited the authority of those in Nazareth who could not accept His mission or who responded with negative judgments such as, "Isn't this the carpenter's son?"

Picture a pyramid with God's words about you and your purpose at the top and everyone else's opinion below that. Perhaps you have some good friends or a pastor who is cheering you on. Their opinions can go right up there below God's opinion. As you work down toward the lower part of the pyramid, you should be thinking about the relationships you have and deciding where in the pyramid of authority they belong.

Finally, make sure you place the voice(s) of your past failures and the limitations of your age, culture, gender, economic status and any other limitations down on the bottom of the pyramid. Choose to limit their influence on your dream. Once you have done this as a purposeful exercise, you will be more prepared to deal with anything that comes your way.

When you encounter people's words or the memories of past circumstances that try to push you off of your dream, you can activate your internal hierarchy of authority. You can put those words and events where they belong—at the bottom of the pyramid where they have little to no authority to speak to your identity or your future.

3. Make an announcement about your mission, and keep announcing it.

Jesus took ownership of His mission and announced it boldly. When you announce your mission, you, too, will find yourself taking ownership of it. You may never have thought about it, but we live on a planet that functions primarily through words. God created the whole universe by making announcements with His words, and those words gave form and structure to His dream for man.

It says in the book of Hebrews, "By faith we understand that the universe was created by the word of God, so that what is seen was not made out of things that are visible" (Hebrews 11:3). God's words began to vibrate in the heavens, and they created the earth, sky, water, animals and people. God made His announcements for this planet starting with, "Let there be light" (Genesis 1:3), and He followed that up with 929 chapters of the Old Testament over thousands of years until His dream to send a Savior was complete.

When you announce your dream as God did, you release the pressure on the inside so that it can dominate on the outside and frame up your dream. This process is like a house being framed up by a carpenter. Your words go forth and give structure and form to what is in your heart. As you speak, you release the powerful presence of the Holy Spirit within you with His supernatural creative power to bring your dream to pass in the earth.

What an empowering thought! As you learn to use your words with intention, you can build up your courage and frame up your future purposely. You do not need to feel defeated and deflated whenever your dream gets a little fuzzy or you start to sense opposition to your dream. God has given you a way to increase and release your courage whenever you need it.

Whether it is decreeing God's word over your dream on a daily basis, telling your close friends about the vision God has given you or watering your dream in prayer, you can use your words to dominate in the Spirit world. This can happen regardless of what is going on in your circumstances.

Paul described this in the book of Ephesians this way: "And do not get drunk with wine, for that is debauchery, but be filled with the Spirit, addressing one another in psalms and hymns and spiritual songs, singing and making melody to the Lord with your heart" (Ephesians 5:18–19). That statement—be filled with the Spirit—is two Greek words: *plērousthe* (to make full)[7] and *pneumati* (wind and spirit).[8] Paul is calling you to pump up the pressure of the Spirit within by using the declarative words of your mouth in psalms, hymns and spiritual songs. This is why we feel our most courageous and bold during times of corporate worship. We are not only declaring what God says about us, we are literally pumping ourselves up (*plērousthe*) with the wind of the Spirit (*pneumati*).

God has invited you to move past the baskets of age and identity. He has invited you to partner with Him to go deep to remove any ungodly beliefs that are holding you back and to create an internal hierarchy of opinions and authority as Jesus did. When you complete this internal work, you will be ready to announce your dream and to scatter your enemies. You will have received an understanding of how to find and sustain courage. And while false identity messages are the biggest thieves of our courage, God has promised to deliver us from all of our fears. Keep this in mind as we confront in our next chapter, "Breaking Free and Shining Brightly," the three remaining baskets that can hold back our dreams.

> *Courage is when the pressure on the inside is greater than the pressure on the outside.*

Questions for Journaling or Discussion

1. Make a list of any ungodly beliefs and fears that are in the way of your dream. To do this, complete these sentences, and identify as many fears and beliefs that come to mind.

   - I am afraid that _____ will hold me back from my dream.
   - I am afraid that I am too _____ to complete my dream.

- I am afraid I do not have enough _____ for my dream.
- I am afraid that if I step out into my dream, _____ will happen.

As you do this exercise, ask God to show you those fears and beliefs for which you need to receive inner healing. A simple way to help you decide if this is necessary is to identify if you have a strong, painful memory or emotion that is attached to the fear or belief. If this is the case, take time with a trusted prayer minister who is experienced in this type of healing to help you work toward wholeness.

2. Draw a pyramid on a piece of paper and write God's name at the top of the pyramid. Then make a list of the people, besides God, who you want to have speak into your identity. Place their names just below His name toward the top of the pyramid. Now place the names of those who may have a negative influence on your dream at the bottom, along with any past experiences or old labels that you have carried that may limit your courage. Hang up your pyramid where you can see it and remind yourself about creating an internal hierarchy.

3. From the above exercise make a list of both your cheering squad and the ones who may squash your dream. Pray about how to respond to each of those groups of people as you move forward.

6

Breaking Free and Shining Brightly

Nor do people light a lamp and put it under a basket . . .

*O*nce you have settled any ungodly beliefs or negative identity messages, you are ready to break out from under any other baskets that have been holding you back. I want you to picture yourself under a basket that is in the way of everything that God has called you to do. You have passed your identity tests and have come into a fuller understanding of your value, your purpose and your mission. You are boldly announcing your assignment to the heavens and the earth, and you are feeling more courage and strength than ever before.

It is time for any remaining issues that are holding you back to be removed. While the baskets of age and identity will hold you back from even beginning, the baskets we will now look at will try to hold you back once you have started to pursue your dream. Sometimes you will not even know they are there until you try to break free. Only then do you realize that you have been hindered. Now that you have begun to find your courage, let's allow that courage to do its work and break you free so that you are truly without apology as you step up into the dream God has given you.

The Basket of Intimidation and the Fear of Failure

In his book *Failing Forward*, John Maxwell said, "The difference between average people and achieving people is their perception of and response to failure."[1] This truth is essential to understand if you are going to succeed at your dream. If you are afraid of failure and are only willing to take a risk when you can guarantee success, then you will be unable to launch and sustain your dream.

Every great entrepreneur, inventor and world changer encounters failure along the path to success. Thomas Edison made thousands of attempts at the light bulb before he experienced success. He once said, "I have not failed 10,000 times—I've successfully found 10,000 ways that will not work."[2]

This is a perfect illustration of how you need to approach your dream and get out from under the basket of intimidation and fear of failure. You will have missteps and things that do not go the way you planned—so you should be prepared to have some failures along the way. If you catastrophize those failures, you will give them the power to shut you down or release an atmosphere of intimidation against you as you try to move forward.

It is important for you to learn how to reframe your missteps as feedback rather than failure. Like Thomas Edison or any other inventor, I want you to see your dream as a wonderful adventure and an experiment in which God has invited you to partner with Him. He will be with you in both the successes and the missteps. My own experience has been that I have learned more from my failures than I have from my successes.

Overcoming setbacks gives you strength and causes you to be sure that God has called you into the dream He has given you. To persevere past a failure, you must go to God for the wisdom to sort it out. When you do that and receive a breakthrough, it will be obvious that it was God who moved on your behalf. This not only glorifies Him, but it deepens your union with Him and keeps you humble. The apostle Paul said in a letter to the Corinthians, "But we have this treasure in jars of clay, to show that the surpassing power belongs to God and not to us" (2 Corinthians 4:7).

God does not expect you to have it all figured out or to have everything perfect. He simply invites you to partner with Him. He wants you to walk closely with Him through every success or failure along the way and to use your dream to glorify Him in the ways that you can.

Now, let's talk about intimidation. Intimidation is often tied to the fear of failure and can create an atmosphere that keeps you from moving forward on the path to your dream. Courage is the answer to intimidation. In order to release your courage to defeat intimidation, you simply need to do one thing: When intimidation comes against a step you are about to take, choose to take the step anyway. Make a quality decision to step into your dream regardless of the pressure that is out there to stop you.

Once you have decided to move past it, the courage and light inside of you will dispel intimidation. I like to say that the devil is like a nagging teenager who is trying to wear you down. With the devil, however, the stakes are higher. It is not a trip to McDonald's or the keys to the car that he is after—he is after your confidence and courage. He is after the seed of your dream before it grows too big for him to stop.

Yet the principle is the same. Once a teenager knows that you have decided that the matter is settled, he will give up his campaign of trying to get what he wants. This is exactly the way it works with intimidation that is released against you to stop your dream. Once the devil knows that you have decided to ignore the intimidation and do what God says no matter what, he has no more cards to play. He will back away, which allows you to move forward into the next stage of your plan. The Bible describes this process of defeating intimidation. "So submit to [the authority of] God. Resist the devil [stand firm against him] and he will flee from you" (James 4:7 AMP)

Overcoming setbacks gives you strength and causes you to be sure that God has called you into the dream He has given you.

The Basket of Avoiding Endings

Again and again I have watched people miss out on opportunities to launch their dreams because they could not move out of the season they were in and into the new thing that God had for them. Like a pile of warm puppies in a basket, we like to stay attached to those around us. We like to be comfortable. If a puppy is taken out of the basket, he cries and longs to get right back to where he was. You, too, may struggle with being able to break free from the roles and relationships that are known and comfortable.

You may feel disloyal or afraid to tell your leader that a new door has opened for you and that it is time for you to move on.

Also, the people around you may have placed a false ceiling over you or expectations on you that serve their interests more than yours. If you cannot navigate an ending to the season you are in, you could be held back from what you are truly called to do.

Over the years I have met women who were CEOs of large corporations Monday through Friday. On Sundays, however, their churches would only allow them to work in the kitchen or to teach Sunday school. Often this was dictated by the doctrinal viewpoint of their denomination regarding the roles of women in the Church. The women were relegated to these areas of service regardless of whether they felt called to those roles. These churches missed out on the powerful leadership abilities of the women in their midst whose obvious gifts, abilities and potential remained largely untapped.

Some people I have met have been made to feel guilty for even considering giving up a role or responsibility they have held for years. They were stuck in situations that no longer gave them joy and fulfillment, but they simply kept going because they did not want to rock the boat and therefore never moved into the new. Others were woven so deeply in friendship and commitment where they had been for many years that the upward call of God—which would have taken them away from these relationships—felt more like a wrenching and tearing than a promotion. They stayed in order to avoid the pain of that tearing away.

In all of these cases, people needed to experience an ending of their current season in order to be able to move into their dream. The same is true for you. What gave you joy years ago may now be unsatisfying. Your potential has outgrown your current assignment, and that assignment is no longer in alignment with your destiny. In order to step into the new, you will need to navigate leaving the old behind.

I like the words of Solomon as he speaks to this issue. "To every thing there is a season, and a time to every purpose under the heaven" (Ecclesiastes 3:1 KJV).

Finding Time For Your Dream

In our busy, fast-paced society, finding the time for your dream can feel elusive. If all you do is think about your dream—whether your dream is to write a book or to launch a business—it will only be a daydream. You need to take action to make it a real dream. To do that, you will need to carve out the time to pursue it. This means taking a hard look at what you are giving your time to right now and assessing whether or not the activities you are participating in are still in alignment with your dream and your new season. And this assessment will often reveal the need for some necessary endings.

In my Dreams Take Flight coaching weekends, I ask each attendee to complete a pie chart that depicts what they are giving their time to. As my participants complete the chart, I can always feel a shift in the atmosphere of the room. It becomes quiet, intense and reflective. Some participants have an aha moment where they understand why they have not been able to find time for their dream. They are able to recognize the many other commitments they have given their time to, some of which were not really necessary.

Some participants become angry or upset as they realize that they have been functioning for years in a role that they no longer hold a passion for. Others have to confront the fact that they are serving another person's cause, and unless they bring about an end to their involvement, they will never find the time to pursue their own dream.

Participants may begin to experience a bit of anxiety as they consider the conversations they will need to have with a leader or organization in order to end their commitment. They almost always come to the conclusion that an ending of some kind is necessary for them to move forward.

Endings are a necessary part of life. If we did not have the ability to end things, we would be married to the first person we dated, and we would still be working at our first job. Yet so often people are stuck and dissatisfied in life because they do not know how—or are afraid—to bring about an ending.

Dr. Henry Cloud, in his book *Necessary Endings*, said:

> Being alive requires that we sometimes kill off things in which we were once invested, uproot what we previously nurtured, and tear down what we built for an earlier time. Refraining, giving up, throwing away, tearing down, hating what we once cherished—all are necessary.[3]

He also says, "Without the ability to end things, people stay stuck, never becoming who they are meant to be, never accomplishing all that their talents and abilities could afford them."[4]

For there to be anything new, the old needs to go. Businesses let go of outdated products and strategies. People move to larger homes because the ones they are in are too small or no longer meet their needs. Sometimes, relationships need to end because they are dysfunctional and hold us back from where we want to go. We may also have personal habits and behaviors that need to end because they are toxic to others or destructive to ourselves and our dreams.

Imagine for a moment that you are standing in your dream. Who is the person that you need to be to stand in that dream? Is there anything that you are doing now that would not be a good fit? Who is with you in the dream? Who is not? How are you spending your time?

Finally, what needs to end for you to be able to step into the dream?

Why We Struggle with Endings

You may know that you need to bring about an ending yet still struggle to bring it about. As I have worked with many people on their dreams, I have learned a lot about why we have trouble with endings. Here are a few reasons:

- We are afraid of the unknown.
- We fear confrontation.
- As Christians, we are taught to never give up hope. This keeps us from confronting things that have been long over.
- We are afraid of the sadness that might be associated with an ending.
- We do not know the right words to use to break away.
- We have had too many painful endings in our journey through life; therefore, we avoid them.
- We think of an ending as a failure.
- We are comfortable and used to our situation—even if we are unfulfilled or unhappy.

This chapter is about courage, and it will take courage for you to bring about an ending. It is worth it in every case, as it frees you to fully pursue your dream without the hindrances of false ceilings, other's expectations, misplaced loyalty or over-commitment. In order to help you end well, I want to share with you the signs of looming transition. These signs will help you recognize when an ending is necessary. Then I will give you some keys on how to end well.

Signs of Looming Transition

If you relate to several of the statements below, it is likely that transition is looming and an ending to your current role or relationship is necessary.

- That which once fueled your passion now drains you.
- You feel that your time is being squeezed.
- You find yourself engaging in time-wasting escapism rather than being fully present.
- You begin to feel critical about things you formerly had grace for. This is your subconscious mind beginning to gather evidence in your heart against the person, place or position as a fuel to help you break away.
- You finally realize that some things and people will never change, and you move from anger and evidence gathering to the recognition that you have outgrown the company, relationship or partnership.
- You begin to get dreams, glimpses and desires for another way of life.
- Your finances dry up for your current assignment.
- Favor lifts off of your current assignment.
- As you begin to consider the ending, excitement and fire ignites within you. Eventually, this excitement for the future becomes stronger than the fear of staying the same.
- God begins to bring multiple confirmations to the steps of faith you are taking.
- Opportunity begins to open up in front of you.
- You sense that His favor is on the new endeavor.

Keys to Ending Well

In the Bible, God is called the Alpha and Omega, the beginning and the end (see Revelation 22:13). We serve a God who not only begins something but completes it. The Bible is full of examples of beginnings and endings, and I believe God wants you to know how to end well. Here are some keys to help you navigate a necessary ending and find the courage to get out from under this basket that has been holding you back for too long.

- Once you have recognized the call to the new and the signs of transition, pray and ask God for confirmation and timing. When you ask God for confirmation, He will bring it, because He is with you in your dream.
- Seek wise counsel from advisors who are outside of the situation and who would have nothing to gain or lose if you were to leave.
- Never abandon your post simply because you are afraid of the conversation that is needed to bring about an ending.
- At the right time, meet with your current boss, team leader or pastor and let them know of your plans. Be sure you have prayed it through and are certain about your ending. If they sense that you are not clear about your need for an ending, you might find them negotiating with you to stay.
- Make the transition as positive as possible. Let go of the criticisms that have arisen during the transition, and thank your former leader/partner for the good that they have sown into you. The time to call for change is not as you are going out the door. If you could have influenced them to change, you would have already. It is my experience that it is best to let love cover the multitude

of failings that you may have seen along the way (see 1 Peter 4:8).

- Work on a plan with your boss, partner, leader or pastor to transition out of your role by raising up at least one person to fill that role. In doing so, you have the opportunity to leave a legacy. I always coach people to raise up their replacement right from the start if they can.

- Sometimes you transition out of a role, but not out of the company or organization. You do not necessarily need to leave everything. Sometimes you just need to adjust your role. This does not always work out well, however. It can be hard for a powerful leader to step to the side and let someone younger or less experienced lead while remaining in the organization. People will still look to the more experienced leader, and this can cause a lot of complications. So you need to be led by the Holy Spirit and have a strong plan if you stay but change your role.

- Be prepared to straddle two seasons and assignments for a short time during your transition. Ask God and others for grace and understanding as your time and energy are squeezed.

- Seek the leading of God for the details of your transition and ask Him for the gift of faith to believe for finances and anything else you will need to launch your dream. When it is time to transition, get fully out—not half out—of the boat in faith. It is time to step out into your dream all of the way!

- Leave through the front door (so to speak) whenever possible, with celebration, prayer and people cheering you on as they see the hand of God accelerating you into your dream.

- Finally, walk away completely and unapologetically without any transition if you realize that you are in a situation that is toxic, abusive, exploitive or illegal. As your first priority, seek the help you need in the form of counseling and support to get healthy and strong.
- Consider making an appointment with a counselor for emotional healing after you leave your old role. This will give you a chance to process any negative emotions or wounds from your last season that you do not want to carry forward into the new.

The Basket of False Humility

American author Marianne Williamson says:

> "Our deepest fear is not that we are inadequate. Our deepest fear is that we are powerful beyond measure. It is our light, not our darkness, that most frightens us." We ask ourselves, Who am I to be brilliant, gorgeous, talented, fabulous? Actually, who are you *not* to be? You are a child of God. Your playing small doesn't serve the world.[5]

Marianne's words confront an issue that has smothered the light of too many Christians—the basket of false humility. We have been taught by our parents, our culture and even our churches that if we enjoy success, we are getting a big head or have a problem with pride. As I described my own journey in chapter 1, I was assaulted with the question "Is it pride or selfish ambition that is making me want to step out and launch my dream?" In Marianne's words, I had to come to see that as a child of God, my playing small was not serving the world.

In order to get out from under this basket of false humility, you, too, will need to confront any self-imposed limits that exist because you are afraid of drawing attention to yourself or of being "too shiny." In the book of Philippians, Paul challenged believers not only to shine, but to shine with such intensity that their lives would be like stars in the sky in contrast to the dark lives of unbelievers. In order for that to happen, you cannot remain hidden or show people only a dulled-down version of who you really are. He said, "So that you may become blameless and pure, 'children of God without fault in a warped and crooked generation.' Then you will shine among them like stars in the sky" (Philippians 2:15 NIV).

It is time to stop disqualifying yourself from greatness, influence, inventions or any other role that God may want to place you in to use your life in a powerful way. He needs you to understand that playing small does not serve the world. And He needs your yes, because He will not force you.

I believe that the Church is experiencing a reformation and a shifting mindset of what it means to be the light of the world. God is calling Christians to boldly step onto the seven mountains (spheres) of influence, which are business, politics, education, media, the family, arts and religion. He needs those who will use their experience, wisdom and passion to lead the way in each of these areas as reformers in our society.

History holds a great example of what can happen when a group of people stop playing small and actually believe that they can make a powerful difference. Such was the case with a group of people known as the Clapham Sect. This was a group of Church of England social reformers who were based in Clapham, London, in the early nineteenth century. Two of their leaders, William Wilberforce and Henry Thornton, championed this group of prominent and wealthy citizens to confront the horrors of slavery and find the courage to fight to see it abolished.

Slavery was not only prevalent in their society, but much of the wealth in their country had been created on the backs of the enslaved. This wealth was held by powerful people throughout England who had a lot to lose if slavery was abolished. Anyone who spoke against slavery was ridiculed and persecuted by powerful leaders who profited from the slave trade. This was not a situation where anything could be gained from playing small.

This group of reformers came to understand that they were called to a cause that was greater than their reputations, their comfort or their desire for privacy. In order to defeat the evil of slavery they had to stick their necks out, be courageous and use their voices in every way that they could.

The results speak for themselves. After many decades of work both in British society and in Parliament, the reformers saw their efforts rewarded with the final passage of the Slave Trade Act in 1807. This act banned slave trade throughout the British Empire. After many additional years of campaigning, they were able to see the total emancipation of British slaves with the passing of the Slavery Abolition Act of 1833.[6] This is what can happen when you remove the limitations around what you give your yes to. God can use your life in an extraordinary way.

I have met many such heroes in my work with Women on the Frontlines. These are average women who gave their yes to God and then saw extraordinary things happen. One such woman is my friend Arleen Westerhof from the Netherlands. She is a brilliant intellectual woman who earned a Ph.D. in chemistry, and then became the founder and director of the Economic Summit and the founder and director of the Center for Economics and Mutuality at Erasmus University in Rotterdam. She now brings together leaders from around Europe every year to create strategies for social justice and change.

Another woman I greatly admire is Janet Porter, an average American woman who was described as so shy that no one believed she could be a public speaker. Her husband challenged her one day with these words: "Why don't you outlaw abortion while you are here?"[7]

In spite of her shyness, Janet went on not only to become an articulate and inspiring speaker, but to author a bill called The Heartbeat Bill that bans abortion the moment a baby's heart starts to beat. At the time of this writing, the bill has been proposed as legislation in 29 states and has been passed into law in 10.

She said that it all began with a belief in the impossible and became reality through a combination of hard work, creativity and persistence. Janet says, "God is the producer of the movie of our life. He is also the director. But He's got an action adventure that would blow Hollywood away."[8]

So it is time for the basket of false humility to go. I want to decree the word *unapologetic* over your life and destiny. I invite you to take ownership of this Scripture as you walk forward: "The wicked flee when no one pursues, but the righteous are bold as a lion" (Proverbs 28:1).

The last two chapters explored the ways we can find the courage we need to break free from anything that is holding us back from our dreams. Finding courage is the internal journey that positions us for the external journey of putting the practical elements of our dream into place. For when we have learned how to find our courage and move past intimidation, expectations and false humility, we are able to develop an action plan in full confidence that we can bring it to pass.

In our next chapter, I will invite you to continue toward the fulfillment of your dream by learning to put the pieces of your dream into a practical plan. To use the metaphor of the Scripture passage we are studying, we will learn to place our light upon a stand.

Questions for Journaling or Discussion

1. What is the thing that intimidates you most about pursuing your dream? What do you need to tell yourself to be able to move past the intimidation and do it anyway?

2. Draw a circle on a piece of paper to create a pie chart that is divided into eight triangles. This pie chart represents the approximate amount of time you have to spend on everything you do. On a separate piece of paper make a list of things that take up your time each week and note the amount of time next to each item on your list.

   Now move the items from your list onto your pie chart, with the time noted next to each activity. You don't need to make it an exact science with each piece of your pie equal. You are simply creating a visual picture of your time commitments.

   Here is the important part of the exercise: Do you see anything on your pie chart that needs an ending?

3. Complete the following exercise: *Imagine standing for a moment in your dream. Who is the person you need to be to stand in that dream? Is there anything you are doing now that would not be a good fit? Who is with you in the dream? Who is not? How are you spending your time? What needs to end in order for you to step into the dream?*

4. What is something that you learned in these last two chapters that you can do every day to build courage for your dream?

7

Positioned to Shine

. . . but on a stand, and it gives light.

In Exodus 25, God gave Moses instructions on how to build a tabernacle where His presence would dwell. The blueprint God gave Moses was incredibly detailed and precise. Included with the tabernacle instructions were directions on how to build a lampstand. These instructions were also highly detailed and specified the exact arrangement of the lamp pieces and the height of the stand.

- Make a lampstand of pure, hammered gold. Make the entire lampstand and its decorations of one piece—the base, center stem, lamp cups, buds and petals.
- Make it with six branches going out from the center stem, three on each side. Each of the six branches will

have three lamp cups shaped like almond blossoms complete with buds and petals.

- Craft the center stem of the lampstand with four lamp cups shaped like almond blossoms complete with buds and petals. There will also be an almond bud beneath each pair of branches where the six branches extend from the center stem.

- The almond buds and branches must all be of one piece with the center stem, and they must be hammered from pure gold. Then make the seven lamps for the lampstand and set them so that they reflect their light forward.

- The lamp snuffers and trays must also be made of pure gold. You will need 75 pounds of pure gold for the lampstand and its accessories.

God concluded these detailed instructions with this statement: "Be sure that everything you make follows the pattern I am showing you here on the mountain" (Exodus 25:40 TLB).

God has called you the light of the world, and He has said that your light belongs on a stand rather than under a basket. Just like the light in the tabernacle, God wants your light to be planned and positioned for success and maximum impact. In the same way that God gave Moses a detailed blueprint and instructions for the tabernacle, I believe He also wants you to receive the practical details and blueprint for your dream.

Generally speaking, the Church has been weak when it comes to equipping people for their dreams. Sunday sermons are big on inspiration, but they often do not spend as much time teaching people about the practical details that are necessary to be able to succeed in some of the realms of influence that we looked at earlier in this book: education, government, media, arts and entertainment, business, family and religion.

I remember the steep learning curve and confusion I experienced when God called me into the realm of media to film some high-quality teaching materials for women. I was aware that the audience I hoped to reach was watching shows like *Oprah*, which were filmed as high-level productions. I knew that this was what I had to compete with for women's time and attention. Yet I had no idea where to begin, and there was no training available through the Church to help me.

Thankfully, some churches are now shifting their mindsets and are offering training sessions on topics such as media, how to run for politics or how to break into the arts—but we still have a long way to go.

My hope is that over the next couple of chapters I can teach you how to develop a detailed plan for your dream that will position you for maximum success. That way, you will be ready as God opens the doors for you to shine your light.

In my years of life coaching, I have found that simple formats are the easiest for people to use to tap into their thoughts and desires; therefore, I have developed a planning outline that works across the board for almost any dream. I call this outline "Putting the *T*s in Your Opportunity." Make sure that you have a pen and some paper ready to use as worksheets, because I want to teach you how to create a framework and blueprint for your dream. I want to show you five *T*s that will help you to successfully plan and execute your dream in practical ways. These *T*s are the *tasks*, *tools*, *targets*, *teams* and *timelines* that are necessary for any opportunity to succeed.

It is not enough to have a vague idea that God will work everything out somehow. You can see from looking at God's interaction with Moses regarding the tabernacle that He cares deeply about details. Picture a road that represents success.

On either side of the road are two ditches that will steal your success. One of the ditches represents a lack of planning, and the other represents fear and doubt.

We have spent a good portion of this book developing your faith for your dream and pulling you out of the ditch of fear and doubt. Now let's make sure that you are not in the ditch of *having no plan* so that you are positioned well on the road to a completed dream.

As you work through this chapter and begin to develop the blueprint for your dream, you may be surprised at how much research there is to do and how many tasks go onto your list. If you feel a little overwhelmed, just step back and work on one section at a time. Remind yourself that what separates the dreams that succeed from the ones that fail is the work you are doing right now. In the words of Jesus, you are counting the cost so that the seed of your dream receives everything it needs to thrive and succeed (see Luke 14:28).

Opportunity

Before we begin to identify the tasks, tools, timelines, teams and targets for your dream, let's talk about identifying your opportunity. An opportunity itself is not your dream. A business or ministry could provide many different opportunities over the years. So while your core mission and your *why* will stay the same, your opportunities will change over time. Each opportunity will need different tasks, tools and timelines.

If you do not have an opportunity open to you for your dream right now, you may need to create your own opportunity. While creating your own opportunity may not sound as spiritual as having one handed to you, sometimes it simply means that God is speaking to you as He spoke to Moses—to build from the ground up.

1. Are there any opportunities open to me right now to launch my dream?

Perhaps you have been offered an opportunity to take a new role, and that is why you have picked up this book. If you have an opportunity already in front of you, write out a description of it on your worksheet. Include *where* the opportunity will take place so that you have it at the forefront of your mind as you continue through these next two chapters.

2. If no opportunity or open door exists for my dream, how can I create my own?

As I said, this is not less spiritual. In fact, it takes real faith to build from the ground up, and God loves initiators. The Bible is full of stories about people who got their breakthrough because they reached out to take hold of their dream, or they left behind what they knew to follow courageously what God was showing them. One of these people, for example, was the woman with the issue of blood.

> And behold, a woman who had suffered from a discharge of blood for twelve years came up behind him and touched the fringe of his garment, for she said to herself, "If I only touch his garment, I will be made well." Jesus turned, and seeing her he said, "Take heart, daughter; your faith has made you well." And instantly the woman was made well.
>
> Matthew 9:20–22

This woman saw an opportunity to fulfill her dream of healing, and she literally reached out and grabbed it. Notice that she created a plan: "If I only touch his garment, I will be made well." She declared this plan to herself, she acted on the plan and she got her desired result.

Abraham is another example. He received only one statement of direction from God:

> Now the LORD said to Abram, "Go from your country and your kindred and your father's house to the land that I will show you. And I will make of you a great nation, and I will bless you and make your name great, so that you will be a blessing."
>
> Genesis 12:1–2

Notice that God told Abraham that if he would step out in obedience to pursue the dream, God would show him where to go. Each opportunity that is attached to your dream will have a location. Whenever I have had to create my own opportunity, I have also asked myself some specific questions that have helped me to identify the *where*.

In 2009 when I decided to create a film series for women, I knew we would need a space in which we could film. I made some calls to inquire about renting local studio space, as we had several organizations in our city that had space available for rent. I was told that the cost to rent a studio would be $1,000 per day! I had sixteen lessons planned for my teaching series, so I was looking at a bill of $16,000 just for the space to film. This price did not include the cost of the film equipment we would need. That amount was totally out of reach for me; therefore, I had to consider other options. I prayed and asked God for wisdom and direction. The book of James says, "If any of you lacks wisdom, let him ask God, who gives generously to all without reproach, and it will be given him" (James 1:5).

God answered my prayer for wisdom. A couple of days later I woke up with the thought that the space I needed was right in front of me. I would use our own large and beautiful home to film the series at no cost. Even though I had never seen a Christian teaching series filmed that way, I believed that this was what God was showing me. This idea was confirmed within a week when my husband and I went to church and a visiting prophet called us to the front of the church. He told us that he had a message from God.

He said, "I see you looking at some plans for your home, and you are asking yourselves, 'Will this work, can we do this?' And God says to you that He has written the word *gateway* over your home, and many who would never go to a church will come into to the Kingdom through your home."

So we began filming in our home with a group of women sitting around the fireplace discussing the concepts of identity and God's plan for women. And the beauty of this was that when the series was finished, everyone said that it was particularly engaging because it was like being invited to a home Bible study.

Look around for a space that is available and within reach to use as your opportunity to launch your dream. I have seen God supply what was needed time and time again.

A few years back I launched a business called Encounter Weight Loss. I wanted to shine my light in the area of helping women lose weight because I knew that so many women struggle in this area. The *where* of my opportunity was the lower level of a church, simply because I could use the space at very little cost. Yet God had so much more in mind for His Kingdom.

Many of the women who joined my weight loss program found themselves entering a church for the first time in their lives. This, in turn, led to some of them joining the church and becoming committed Christians. Do not underestimate the ways that God can use whatever is in your hand or within your reach to launch your dream—even if you have to use an unlikely space.

When Moses had doubts about whether he would have the ability to offer to Pharaoh and the Israelites a sign that his cause was authentic, God did not ask Moses for something he did not have. He asked Moses for what he *did* have. "Then Moses answered, 'But behold, they will not believe me or listen to my voice, for they will say, "The LORD did not appear to you."' The LORD said to him, 'What is that in your hand?' He said, 'A staff'" (Exodus 4:1–2). God used what was in Moses' hand to launch his dream. He can do that for you, too.

3. Is there anything within my hands or within my reach?

On your worksheet I want you to write out the mission statement for your dream that we developed in chapter 3. This is your "I will_____, because _____" statement.

Once you have written that down on your worksheet, consider what it will look like when you launch your dream. I will be asking you to identify many things you need for your dream when we look at the Tools section, but for now, I want you to consider *where* you will do it.

Can you develop and practice it from home, or do you need a different kind of space? Describe what you think you need. Is there anywhere available to you where you can access the type of space that you need? Jot down possible spaces, contacts, connections and anything else God brings to mind that might help you. If you are certain that you can develop and launch your dream out of your home, write down where in your home your dream space will be and anything you will need to do to make that space functional for working on your dream.

Pray for wisdom and ask God to show you what is in your hand or within your reach that you can use as a space for your opportunity. I believe you will be amazed at how God can answer your prayer.

Tasks

There is an old saying that goes, "If you fail to plan, you plan to fail." This applies specially to identifying the tasks associated with completing your dream. Jesus made the following observation about following through on our heart's intent:

> "For which of you, desiring to build a tower, does not first sit down and count the cost, whether he has enough to complete it? Otherwise, when he has laid a foundation and is not able to finish, all who see it begin to mock him, saying, 'This man began to build and was not able to finish.'"
>
> Luke 14:28–30

So if you want to complete your dream successfully, a list of tasks will be necessary.

We already looked at your first task: Find a location for my dream. Recognize that one task may have sub-tasks. Finding a location may be a goal that will require several actionable tasks. These could be phoning contacts, researching prices, booking a space and signing a contract.

Then, once you have the space, you may set a new goal, such as have the space set up and ready to go each week. This goal will also have multiple tasks attached to it. Goals that are followed by lists of tasks needed to reach those goals is a simple way to outline your dream and count the cost, as Jesus said, to see if you are ready to complete it.

The following are some aspects that are involved in most dreams. Go through the list and identify your goals and tasks. You will find yourself coming back to this task list and adding to it as you work through the other Ts. This is all part of the process to make your dream shine and come to life.

Research Goals and Tasks

Make a list of tasks that are necessary to research and educate yourself about your dream. This list should include studying existing models that are already out there. As you study other models, prayerfully consider the way that your dream fits into the unique culture and society in which you are living, and plan accordingly.

If your dream is a business, you will need to research the marketplace. If your dream is to run for politics, you will need to research the issues that are facing your constituents and the platforms of the other candidates. If your dream is in the area of media, you will need to research the necessary equipment and training that will be required to launch your project. If your dream is in the realm of family, you will want to research the key issues that are facing families and what resources are available. If your dream is in the area of arts and entertainment, you will need to research the ways you can launch that dream in your community. In the book of Numbers, Moses sent out men to research what was ahead of the Israelites on their journey.

> See what the land is like. See if the people who live in it are strong or weak, and if they are few or many. Find out if the land they live in is good or bad. See if the cities they live in are open or if they have walls. Find out if the land is rich or poor, and if there are trees in it or not.
>
> Numbers 13:18–20 NLV

The same will hold true for you. In any area in which God has called you to dream, spending the time to research the realm of that dream will pay big dividends by preparing you for what is ahead.

Manpower Goals and Tasks

After you read the Team section in the next chapter, you will identify the team needed to bring your dream to pass. In addition, each person on your team will have a job description and a list of tasks. But for now, it will be helpful for you to make a rough list of manpower tasks that you will need to complete in pursuit of your dream. This will help you immensely when you get to the Team section and you are asked to narrow down your tasks to specific roles.

Financial Goals and Tasks

Make a list of tasks that will be necessary to discover the financial costs associated with your dream. This will include things such as pricing out the location for your dream, researching the cost of manpower, identifying banks or other places to raise capital, writing a business plan, meeting with investors, and researching the costs of supplies and advertising and licensing. Ask God to help you count the financial cost of your dream and all of the associated financial tasks.

If you do not know how to write a business plan, there are several free online tools available that will guide you through the process in a style that will be accepted by a bank. Simply do an online search for "free business plan template" and some options will come up.

Personal Development Goals and Tasks

Make a list of personal training tasks that you will need to be proficient in to launch your dream. These may include post-secondary education, media and film training or classes to improve your computer skills. List any skill you lack currently that you feel will be necessary to accomplish your dream.

In addition to listing these practical development tasks, ask yourself if there are any spiritual development tasks or healing tasks that you will need to complete. We spent the first part of this book talking about faith, courage and identity needs that have an impact on your dream. If you believe that you need further development in one of these areas, then set out goals and tasks that relate to that specific emotional or spiritual need.

Prayer Goals and Tasks

While this may not be found on a typical business plan, I encourage you to set prayer as a priority to help you accomplish your dream. Think of prayer times as meeting with the most important team member of your dream team. If you schedule these prayer times as priority tasks, they will remain with you. They will keep you centered and directed by God as your dream grows. This is especially important if you are coordinating a team of people in your endeavor.

My ministry, Women on the Frontlines, meets twice per week for prayer. We approach this task with joy and intentionality and attribute our success to the favor, direction and break-throughs that have come out of these prayer meetings. The Bible addresses this important topic in the book of Proverbs. "Commit your works to the LORD [submit and trust them to Him], and your plans will succeed [if you respond to His will and guidance]" (Proverbs 16:3 AMP).

Tools

Tools are the equipment and resources that you will need to have on hand to bring your vision to pass. These can include everything from the tools of a trade, such as mechanical tools or filming tools, to a stapler and paper for handouts.

When I am working on the plan for a new dream, I like to "empty" my mind of every tool (piece of equipment) that I can think of that relates to my dream. If a stapler is the first thing that comes to mind, I write it down and get it out of the way. I leave a scratch pad open for days as I continue to write down tools. As I ponder the vision, I increase my task list.

I might need, for example, a video camera as a tool for my dream, so I write that down as a goal. I then add several tasks to list. Goal: Get a video camera. Tasks: Research video cameras, price video cameras, raise money for video camera selected and purchase video camera.

Once I have completed my list of tools that I will need, I ask myself an important question. This question always moves me into the realm of faith, and it has often brought about supernatural answers to the needs attached to my dream. The question I ask is the same as the one God asked Moses: What do I have in my hand? You see, with almost every dream that I have launched, I have had no money or equipment to start with. As I have learned to ask that question, however, one of the two following things has always happened to bring forward movement to my dream.

Despise Not Small Beginnings

Sometimes God has revealed to me that I have something in my hand that I can start with. Like Moses and his staff, we often have something. It might not be state-of-the-art, but it will do the job. I learned this important lesson from my parents when I was a young girl. They decided that they wanted to add a basement to our 1950s house that only had a dirt crawlspace below it.

My parents did not have money for a contractor or expensive equipment. What they did have was a pile of shovels and a desire to complete their dream. There is an old saying that you can eat an elephant one bite at a time. Well, as I came to see, you can also dig a basement one shovelful at a time.

I remember vividly my mom handing me down through the hole under our kitchen sink to my dad who was in the partly dug basement. With construction lights on long cords hanging from the ceiling and a conveyor belt of mud going out of one small window, I was handed a child-sized shovel and got to "help" dad accomplish something that seemed impossible: removing tons of mud one shovelful at a time to accomplish a dream.

That experience left an indelible mark on me. I learned that if you are humble and willing to work hard using what you have in your hand, you can accomplish things that others would scoff at. I have learned to use whatever I have at hand to show God that I am serious about the dream, and that has always paid off with divine favor and provision. I may have started with a shovel, but I have always ended up with the best that God could give me as He has honored my faithfulness.

Too many people miss out on their dream because they are prideful and do not want to be seen with a (metaphorical) shovel in their hand. They want to start at the top with the latest state-of-the-art equipment. Well, if that is you, I would encourage you to humble yourself as you start your dream.

After you make your list of tools, ask God to show you if you have anything that you can use to bridge the gap to get you started until you have more. My mentor, Patricia King, started her television show in her kitchen with an inexpensive camera and two construction lights. She now has a state-of-the-art studio with equipment that most media people only dream of having.

The Bible tells the story of Zerubbabel, who was called by God to rebuild the temple in Jerusalem that lay in ruins. Those who rebuilt the temple faced an overwhelming task. Yet God spoke to Zerubbabel though an angel and said:

> "This is what the LORD says to Zerubbabel: *It is not by force nor by strength, but by my Spirit, says the LORD of Heaven's Armies.* Nothing, not even a mighty mountain, will stand in Zerubbabel's way; it will become a level plain before him! And when Zerubbabel sets the final stone of the Temple in place, the people will shout: 'May God bless it! May God bless it!' Then another message came to me from the LORD: "Zerubbabel is the one who laid the foundation of this Temple, and he will

complete it. Then you will know that the LORD of Heaven's Armies has sent me. *Do not despise these small beginnings, for the LORD rejoices to see the work begin*, to see the plumb line in Zerubbabel's hand."

Zechariah 4:6–10 NLT, emphasis added

Sacrifice Releases Your Faith

The other thing that I have experienced when I have needed tools and have asked God to show me what is in my hand is that He has told me to *sacrifice* something that I had right in front of me in order to bring the dream to fruition. I sometimes wonder what God thinks as He listens to our prayers for provision while we sit in our homes that are overflowing with unused and unwanted possessions that could be easily sold to launch our dreams.

If you are humble and willing to work hard using what you have in your hand, you can accomplish things that others would scoff at.

Let me tell you a couple of stories about this topic, because I want to inspire you with how God can move on your behalf if you are willing to sacrifice. You see, there is something about sacrifice that moves God's heart. Sometimes this even means liquidating the life you had before so that there can be no going back.

One of my favorite stories about this is found in the gospel of Mark. Bartimaeus was a blind beggar who heard that Jesus was walking near where he sat and begged for money. During Jesus' time on the earth the government had regulations for beggars. If a person had a valid reason to be begging—such as because they were blind—they would be given a beggar's coat from the government to show that they were not scamming anyone.

It is not hard to imagine that Bartimaeus had a dream of having his sight restored. I bet that he often sat and dreamed about what it would be like to see. So when Bartimaeus heard that Jesus was near, he began to cry out in a loud voice, "Jesus, Son of David, have mercy on me" (Mark 10:47 NKJV). The disciples told him to be quiet, but Jesus heard him and called him over. The disciples said to him:

> "Be of good cheer. Rise, He is calling you." *And throwing aside his garment, he rose and came to Jesus.* So Jesus answered and said to him, "What do you want Me to do for you?" The blind man said to Him, "Rabboni, that I may receive my sight." Then Jesus said to him, "Go your way; your faith has made you well." And immediately he received his sight and followed Jesus on the road.
>
> Mark 10:49–52 NKJV, emphasis added

Notice that Bartimaeus sacrificed his valuable beggar's garment in his determined pursuit of Jesus. Not only was he sacrificing his current means of income, but he was also casting aside the identity of a blind beggar all in one swoop. This released his faith. In response, Jesus said to him, "Your faith has made you well."

God honors sacrifice, and sacrifice releases faith. When you are willing to sacrifice what you have in order to pursue the dream of God, you are placed squarely in the dream. The dream has now cost you something, which draws out faith and determination.

I have seen this in my own life again and again. In 2009 when I set out to film, I needed about $50,000 worth of equipment. My bank balance for the dream was zero, and I did not have any tools in my hand that I could use to film. But I did have an upholstery business that brought in a secondary income stream for my family. For months, I had been trusting God for film equipment and praying for breakthrough. We were set to start filming in about thirty days, and we would need at least one camera to start with.

One day as I prayed, I heard God say to my heart, *What do you have in your hand?* I scanned my life looking for answers and could think of nothing useful. Then it came to me: my secondary business. I knew that if I sold my upholstery equipment, I might make enough for a camera and a few other items—but there would be no going back. It had taken me years to collect the upholstery equipment, and much of it was hard to come by. If I sold it, I would be closing that door of income in my life.

Yet I wanted to obey God. I made a small poster and gave it to a couple of fabric wholesalers in my city. As the weeks leading up to our planned filming went by, I heard from no one. Then less than a week before we were to start, I got a phone call. A man said he would like to come and see my upholstery equipment. I was really excited and waited for him on the appointed day, but he did not come. I had a friend with me who could see my disappointment.

She said, "Don't be moved by what you see. God's got this." I repented internally for my unbelief, and within minutes the phone rang. It was the man who had been interested in the equipment. He told me that he had gotten caught up and could not come to see it. Then something supernatural happened.

He was silent for a moment and then said, "I'll tell you what. I don't need to see your equipment. I will buy it at full price. I am putting a check in the mail to you today and you can deliver it to me whenever you have time." This man had never met me. As unlikely as that sounds, that is what happened.

The check arrived within two days, and we ordered and received our first film camera less than 24 hours before we were set to launch the dream. Many more miracles came after that until we had received over $50,000 worth of Hollywood quality film

Just Getting Started

equipment for a fraction of the cost and in the most unusual ways—but it all started with sacrifice.

Since that time, I have always invited my teams to sacrifice when we are pursuing a dream together. Whether it is the $6,000 for a mission trip that we raised at a yard sale by scouring our homes for both unwanted and dearly loved possessions that we sacrificed for the cause, or by pouring money that we did have into wherever God directed, I have seen time and again that sacrifice will move heaven. If you will do your part, God will do His.

Questions for Journaling or Discussion

1. We explored the idea of creating your own opportunity. What did you find when you looked around your life to see if there was anything at hand or within reach that would be a location for your dream?

2. If you have not found a place for your dream, what kind of place did you identify as you worked on your scratch pad?

3. We looked at tasks in this chapter. For some it can come as a surprise to see how much research needs to go into

140

a dream to make it succeed. What are one or two areas of research that you need to look into before launching your dream?

4. You will need tools for your dream. What are some items that you have on hand that you can use for your dream? Are there any metaphorical shovels (humble tools) that you need to start with until you get better tools? What are they?

5. Is God asking you to sacrifice something that you can pour into the dream? What is it? Does it force you to leave a part of your life behind? If so, what part?

8

Finding Your People

It gives light to all who are in the house.

We have been on a progressive journey through the stages that align with the development of your dream as we have worked through Matthew 5:14–16. The first stage was a recognition that you are the light of the world with unique gifts that God has given you. The second stage was an understanding that it is not God's will for your light to be hidden. The third stage was that your light should be positioned for maximum effectiveness. The fourth stage that we will now look at is that the purpose of this journey is to bring your unique light to people.

For God's treasures are not silver or gold. God's treasures are people. The Bible makes this clear through verses such as "But you are a chosen race, a royal priesthood, a holy nation, a people for his own possession, that you may proclaim the excellencies of him who called you out of darkness into his marvelous light" (1 Peter 2:9).

When God calls us the light of the world, He is inviting us to bring His love and light to the people we are connected with through our dream. The purpose of this is to call them out of darkness and into His marvelous light and wonderful love.

Jesus said, "Nor do people light a lamp and put it under a basket, but on a stand, and *it gives light to all in the house*" (Matthew 5:15, emphasis added). So if we are going to give light to all who are in the house, we will need to identify exactly who it is that is in our house—metaphorically speaking. This will be the target that you put into your opportunity.

Target

My good friend dropped by to visit me on her way back from attending Missionfest, which is a local event that invites ministries to come together and share their mission in a trade show setting with rows of booths, guest speakers and break-out sessions. She seemed a little shaken up.

When I asked her why, she said, "As I was walking down the rows with all the booths, I felt as if there were hundreds of hands reaching out to me crying, 'Help me! Help me!' I ended up feeling totally overwhelmed and uncertain of what to do."

Her experience illustrates an important truth: If you do not identify the target of your dream (who it is for), you may become overwhelmed by the needs and demands of our broken and hurting world. You need to know who is in your house (your realm of influence), as these are the specific people God wants you to have an impact on through your dream.

Who Are the People in Your House, and What Is Their Story?

We all have people who are "in our house." These are the folks who our light reaches through our realm of influence. As you work to identify the people who are the target of your dream, it helps to do two specific things. First, understand what is unique about your dream (business, product, experience or organization), and second, understand what is unique about the people you want to reach.

Let's start by considering your realm of influence. Every person has a group of people with whom they are in contact. This list includes friends, family, church members, those you know through social clubs and outings and those you target specifically to influence through your dream. Some people have a small realm of influence such as a local Bible study or a small business, while some have a large realm of influence such as an international ministry or a large corporation.

It is important to understand that there is not a right or wrong realm of influence, and one is not better than the other. Remember that I said in chapter 1 that God has not called us to exposure but to effectiveness. It is not as important how big the group of people is that you reach. The important thing is that you find a way to reach them effectively. If you want to succeed at your dream, you will need to let go of old mindsets such as bigger is better. Bigger is not necessarily better—it is just bigger. If you only measure success by size and continually try to push for that, you may miss completely what your target audience wants.

Not everyone is attracted to a large business, ministry or cause. Many people are looking for something more intimate that will meet their needs in a personal way. Others prefer the characteristics of a large entity and what it can offer them. Some will want something expensive, while others prefer something affordable. You cannot and should not try to be all things to all people. Your dream is not for everyone. You need to identify your unique positioning that will attract those you want to reach.

To start with, I would like you to complete the simple excise below. See if you can identify where you and your dream fit on a quadrant diagram next to others who are doing something similar. This quadrant exercise will help you identify both yourself and your target people. Your quadrants can contain any combination of words that help you identify your position, such as "fast delivery versus slow delivery," "one-hour church service versus two-hour church service," "female versus male" or "old versus young." Once you understand how to use it, you can go back and try other combinations so that you can fine-tune your understanding of who you are and who your people are. But for now, let's start with "big versus small" and "affordable versus expensive."

To do this exercise, draw a cross on your scratch pad. It should look like a large plus sign (+).

In the top right corner write the word *Big*. In the bottom left corner (diagonally) write the word *Small*.

Now in the top left corner write the word *Expensive*, and in the lower right corner (diagonally) write the word *Affordable*.

Your diagram should appear like this:

Expensive	**Big**
Small	**Affordable**

As you look at your dream, what two characteristics best describe what you want to do or offer? Is your business, ministry, product or experience that you are offering big and expensive or big and affordable? Is it small and expensive or small and affordable? Every dream has an on-ramp that people need to walk so that they can access what is being offered. If the on-ramp is not relatable to who they are, what they can afford or what they really want, they will not access it.

You make choices all of the time about products, stores, experiences and churches. It is not, however, the product, store, experience or church in and of itself that causes you to seek it out. It is also the story that you tell yourself about that product or church that primarily influences your choice.

We tell ourselves stories every day about everything we choose. You can take two jars of the exact same face cream and mark one with a cheap, no-name label and mark the other one with an exclusive and expensive looking label, and people will buy that same cream for different reasons.

One lady will buy the no-name jar of cream because the story she tells herself is, "I am a good steward of money and this is affordable." Another lady will buy the same exact cream but with the high-end label for forty dollars more because the story she tells herself is, "I am worth it, and this extra money spent is necessary to keep me looking young."

The story that we tell ourselves is what advertisers get paid a lot of money to create. In fact, advertisers often say that they do not sell products, but they sell a promise of a better life that is attached to a product. They sell identity messages about who the people are who buy their product.

If we are going to "give light to all who are in the house," we will need to identify exactly who it is that is in our house, metaphorically speaking.

In my organization, Women on the Frontlines, our branding statement is this: "Because every woman wants to make a difference." The implied promise that we are making is that by choosing to be involved with us, you will make a difference in the world. Along with the name of the organization, this branding statement also sends an identity message about being a powerful woman as you make that difference.

You, too, are inviting people into an identity message and a story about themselves when they choose to be involved with you. The more clearly you understand this, the better you will be at reaching your people and expanding your realm of influence. I will give you a few examples to consider as we ponder this together.

> **Business example: Walmart**—Big and Affordable. What promise and identity message does Walmart send? Hint—it is in their branding statement: "Save Money. Live Better." So what stories are the people who shop at Walmart telling themselves?
>
> **Business example: Local, Artisan Jewelry**—Small and Expensive. What promises and identity message does this type of store send? What stories are the people telling themselves when they buy from a small, local artisan?
>
> **Business example: Saks Fifth Avenue, New York**—Big and Expensive. What promises and identity messages does Saks provide their rich shoppers? What stories do you think people are telling themselves as they walk out of Saks in New York with bags of expensive products?
>
> **Business example: Flea Market Crafter**—Small and Affordable. What promises and identity message does the mom send who handcrafts hats and jewelry out of recycled fabric and old brooches? What message is she telling herself when she makes them? What stories are the people telling themselves who buy from her?

You can see as you look at these examples that whatever you create as a dream will not only be unique, but it will draw a specific group of people who are telling themselves a certain story.

"People like us believe, feel, want _____." As you learn to identify the people in your "house" upon whom you are shining your light, you will find that a lot of your work will be centered around understanding your unique message and what your people want.

In order to help you do that well, I will ask you to answer a few more questions. Try to fill in as much information as possible about your message, your product and the people you want to have an impact on. Do extra research as needed.

1. What do you make, create or provide through your dream?

2. Who is it primarily for?
   - gender
   - age
   - ethnicity
   - marital status
   - family size
   - financial status
   - location
   - values
   - political leanings
   - interests
   - lifestyle
   - personality

- purchase history
- experiences that are important to them

3. Who is it not for?

4. How do you hope to reach your people? (in person, advertising, internet, etc.)

5. How much does it cost to buy your product or experience?

6. How does that compare to similar products in the marketplace?

7. What is the promise that your product or service is making to your people?

8. What is the identity message attached to what you have to offer? If you buy this, come to this or join us, you will be_____.

9. Are there problems you solve for your people? If so, what are they?

10. Complete this sentence: People who choose my dream want _____. Jot down as many things as you can think of.

11. How will you measure the success of your dream?

After working to answer all of these questions, try to narrow down the criteria of the target person you want your dream to have an impact on.

The person I want to reach is (describe them) _____.

The story they are telling themselves when they choose my product, organization or experience is_____.

Now use all of the information you have collected to narrow down the ways that you will reach your people. List things like advertisements, in-person contact, curated events, social media, newsletters or anything else you can think of to bring your light to them.

Team

Have you ever seen a sports team that played incredibly well together? Successful sports teams have players who are able to anticipate what their teammate is about to do and position themselves to be in the right place as the ball or puck comes to them. They also understand that it is not all about getting the glory for themselves by hogging the ball. They see that it is about working together for overall success and handling failure together without casting blame.

Your team is the people who help you complete your dream. You may have a large team of many people or a small team with just you and a couple of others. Either way, the quality of people you surround yourself with can make or break your dream. A successful dream will have a successful team behind it, and developing a successful team is not a quick exercise or one-time event.

In order to identify who is needed on your team, go back to your task list and look at all of the tasks needed to complete your dream. Group the tasks together into lists that reflect a job that one person or a small group can do well. A few examples would be financial administration, graphics and design, marketing or hospitality.

Think about all the moving parts of your dream and who will complete those tasks. In the beginning, you might be the primary one to do those tasks due to financial considerations. Even if that is the case, I would still encourage you to make a list of needed team members so that you can invite people into your dream as it grows.

As you look at the task lists you have made, you should be able to begin to write job descriptions for each role. In my years of working with many teams, I have learned some important lessons about building teams. I would like to share some of those lessons with you so that you can learn from my experiences and save yourself some missteps and pain. Here are a few things I have learned over the years about working with a team.

Know Your Team

Each time that I invite a new member onto my team, I set up a two-hour meeting with him or her. During the first hour of that meeting, I ask this person to tell me his or her story. The team member will often ask how far back he or she should go in that story. I always answer, "From as far back as you can remember." Then I listen. I listen to the story, to the way that the person communicates, to the things that he or she highlights as important and to the way that the team member has responded to or has overcome setbacks and challenges throughout his or her journey.

This gives me valuable insight into the history of each of my team members, and it connects our hearts before we even start to work together. It allows each person to feel seen and heard right from the start, which is very important. I have observed that a common cause of people leaving a team is that they feel unheard or invisible.

I also ask my team members to share if they have had any significant financial challenges along the way and, if so, how they resolved them. And I ask them what they believe about giving. This tells me about their past stewardship of resources and helps me see their strengths and weaknesses in this area. This initial meeting is the best investment I can make into future team members. It shows me whether they have a similar spiritual belief system as the rest of our team.

This is a good time for you to ask them what they understand about your dream or cause in which you have invited them to serve. New members may reveal to you that they have a very different goal than you do for what is to be accomplished. Do not choose someone for your team who is going in a different direction than you are going with the hopes that he or she will eventually see it your way. What is more likely to happen is that he or she will cause confusion and dissension in the team due to his or her desire to go a different way.

I always look for character above gifting, because it is much easier for people to learn skills than it is to correct character flaws. I recommend that you try to match the character, personality and commitment level of your volunteers or employees with their role. Ask them what a ten out of ten would look like for their involvement in your dream. You may be surprised at what they share. Some people like to work behind the scenes, and some people like to be up front and leading others.

If your team members are asked to serve in roles for long periods of time that do not fuel their passion, they can become resentful and burned out. Understanding the motivation and desires of your team members is one of the most important things you can put effort into. Investing in this understanding will pay big dividends when it comes to their connection to the dream and their willingness to serve. Too often teams fall apart due to uninformed assumptions and a lack of communication. Do not be that leader. Take the time to know those who labor among you (see 1 Thessalonians 5:12).

Commitment

You should define clearly the commitment and the expectations that accompany what you are asking for. If you need your team members to attend weekly meetings, let them know that that is the expectation. Be very clear about your expectations, and do not be afraid to ask each team member what he or she can bring to the table. Is there a part of the financial burden of the dream that you want them to contribute to? If the answer is yes, then make sure you talk about it. People are not mind readers, and if you do not let your team members know what is expected of them, then you are doing them and yourself a disservice.

It is also very important to determine why they are with you and whether they feel called to serve you and your dream. Do not make the mistake of putting people on your team for sentimental reasons. Just because someone has been a friend for twenty years does not mean he or she will be a great team member. If fact, natural affection and old loyalties can make it harder to confront issues as they come up, and sometimes close friends think the rules do not apply to them.

There is also the issue of addressing the "inherited" team members who might have come along with a role into which you have stepped. These people have loyalties to the leader they served before you. They may compare you to the previous leader and find fault with you. In these circumstances, you will have to work doubly hard to win their trust and confidence.

I recommend that you set up a trial period of working with any inherited team members during the initial meeting that you have. Be clear to communicate that there will be no hard feelings if either party decides this situation is a wrong fit. This will give them an easy way out if they do not believe in the fresh vision you are bringing. Whatever happens, please do not start to compromise or people-please order to keep the inherited ones. That will undermine your confidence and authority, and it will place you on the defensive. It is better to let them move on if they do not click with you. They often do not know why they are still in the room, so to speak, and they will need to work through that in a healthy way if they are to serve with you.

Define how long each team member's commitment will last. Or, if there is a trial period, make sure you book a follow-up meeting to discuss how things are progressing at the end of the trial period. I like to ask my team at Women on the Frontlines to commit to serve for one year at a time. This allows me to count on my team through both the good and difficult times that are experienced throughout each year without wondering if they are committed to seeing it through.

The one-year time frame also leaves room for my team members to move on at the end of the year if their circumstances change. Some people will be with you for a short time, and some may be with you for your entire journey to your dream's completion. We use September to September as our one-year time period so that our team members have time to assess their commitment over the summer, which we have found is less busy. We also have a protocol for how people leave our team. This protocol includes the team member helping us train his or her replacement and us celebrating and blessing the team member as he or she moves on to new assignments in God's Kingdom.

Core Values

With your team, you should define the core values that you will uphold together as a standard to live by. Once you have agreed on the core values, review them together regularly. We discuss one of our core values regularly at our Women on the Frontlines team meeting so that we can keep them before us and stay in agreement on how we have committed to live. I like to have my team members take turns leading a devotion on one of our core values. This helps all of the members take ownership of those values as their own.

When you take the time to define your core values and uphold them as the standard for your team, you will find that those values will provide a framework to use when resolving conflict or when addressing character issues that arise with team members. When your team has agreed to live from a set of core values but a problem surfaces, you can hold up the core value next to the errant behavior and ask your team member to identify the ways that his or her behavior is out of alignment with the core value. This allows the member to have an aha moment, and it is much more effective than lecturing, nagging or trying to make people do as you ask. If you set the bar with excellence, it will create excellence for your team.

Here are the core values we have developed for Women on the Frontlines: healthy communication, humility and servanthood, excellence and diligence, high moral character, being correctable, intimacy with God, grooming and dress, transparency, respect and honor. Each of these core values has a Bible verse attached to it and specific details regarding the expectations that accompany it. If it is important, for instance, that your team has a specific code of conduct when you host events or travel, then I would encourage you to weave that into your core values and communicate clearly about it.

My team's commitment form also contains a list of team responsibilities, such as meeting project deadlines and showing up on time for meetings, as well as reasons that a team member might be removed from our team. If you feel uncomfortable developing guidelines for dismissal, ask your team to help you decide on them. These guidelines and core values protect your whole team, and you will be glad that you have created them if any difficulties arise with a team member.

Communication

Discuss with each team member who they are accountable to and who they need to manage and inform. As a part of our Healthy Communication core value for Women on the Frontlines, we ask team members to respond to messages within 24 hours, even if the reply is a simple "I got it." This way we know they are informed.

As our ministry grew, we moved from using group emails and Facebook Messenger to spending the money to have a team communication app. Switching to using this app was a very positive step for us as a team, because it allowed every conversation to be in one place and easy to find. The app that we use is called Slack, but there are many others you can choose from. Find one that meets your team's needs and keeps your team communications from getting lost in the many digital messages we all receive daily.

As a part of our Healthy Communication value, we have defined the guidelines regarding how we will handle conflict. Our core value is that we deal with each other face-to-face. If we are afraid to do that, we find one other team member to join us for help and assistance. My mentor, Patricia King, showed great wisdom and ministry experience when she interviewed me for my role as the global director for Women on the Frontlines.

She said to me in that meeting, "If there ever comes a point where you are offended by me, I hope you trust me enough to approach me. If for some reason you cannot, then I am assigning _____ as the person you are to go to." Patricia understands a lot about human nature and people's propensity to internalize things rather than communicate. She has built into her organization structured pathways toward healthy resolution for conflict. I have learned a lot from her in this regard.

I have also learned to ask at the end of my calls with Patricia in her role as my mentor, "Patricia, is there anywhere that you can see that I have lacked wisdom or need correction?" I encourage those I mentor to do the same when they meet with me. This invites feedback, builds trust in the relationship and encourages growth. On the other side of this coin, asking your team members for input is also a key to success. If you only lead through giving orders and being in charge, you will not gain truly loyal team members. I like to ask my team for input on every important decision and change that we make so that they have a sense of ownership and feel heard, knowing that they are a valuable part of our team. In return, they show a tremendous amount of honor and respect to me.

Servant Leadership

Jesus said, "You know that the rulers of the Gentiles lord it over them, and their great ones exercise authority over them. It shall not be so among you. But whoever would be great among you must be your servant" (Matthew 20:25–26). Jesus gets right to the heart of the matter when it comes to building a team. Your team is not there to serve you—you are there to serve them. And you are on a team so that you can serve a cause that is greater than yourselves.

As a leader, you can serve your team by inspiring them and keeping the dream alive in them. You can serve them by encouraging them when times are tough and when progress is slow, and by celebrating their efforts and acknowledging their accomplishments in front of others. You can serve them by introducing them as the people they are becoming, and by believing in them more than they even believe in themselves. And you can serve them by praying for them and showing a genuine interest in their lives.

I am very practical in my approach to leadership. Rather than hoping that everything will work out by itself, I like to create or build in anything that I want to see. In practical terms, this means that I schedule weekly meetings with our large team and regular meetings with my team leaders. At the end of each meeting, while our calendars are still in front of us, we book our next meeting. I also stay on Zoom after our big team meeting each week to be available to pray for individual needs that our team members have. Each week a few of our team members stay for prayer. They tell me they feel cared for and protected because of these times that we have built in.

I also like to take the time to craft or select an individual gift for each of my team members at Christmas. This is a way that I can serve and celebrate them, even if it is a financial sacrifice to do so. Many teams fall apart because their leadership fails to do these simple relational steps that serve their members. Most of the ways that I serve my team have been developed because of having had bad experiences in the past as a team member. When one of my mentors said to me, "Wendy, you cannot change another leader, you can only be a different leader yourself," I took it to heart. I try my best every day to aspire to be a servant leader, and I believe that you can, too.

I want to share one final thought on team building. Make sure that you have some mentors and people outside of your organization who speak into your life regularly and to whom you are accountable. If and when any trouble comes to you or your organization, these are people who will be able to offer you wisdom and insight on how to deal with the trial you are experiencing. Their distance will allow them to stay objective without becoming caught up in any drama around the issue. I also always select at least one board member who is not involved in daily operations on my teams. If your financial integrity is ever questioned, this person will be able not only to speak objectively to financial issues, but also to speak to your financial integrity from a position outside of the organization.

Timeline

The final "T" that you need to put into your opportunity is your timeline. This will involve taking all of your tasks and planned meetings and plotting them out on a timeline. When our team does big events, we often get a large roll of craft paper and roll it out across a big conference table. At the end of the paper, we put the date of the event. At the beginning of the paper, we put the current date. Then we begin to plot out in pencil or on Post-it notes everything needed to pull off a successful event. We shuffle tasks as needed until they are all accounted for. A couple of things that will help you with creating successful timelines:

- Do not avoid creating written timelines and handouts. Most people like to have clear direction and organized plans that spell out what is expected of them. It is very hard to follow leaders who fly by the seat of their pants or who make ideas or projects up as they go along. This kind of leader often ends up overwhelmed and can be prone to escalating tension, stress and blame shifting as deadlines draw near and tasks are not completed. I have worked with a few leaders like this on projects. They will say things like "I've got it all up here in my head," when asked for the schedule. I have observed that due to not having a timeline planned they often have trouble delegating and take on too much themselves. This can lead to a looming deadline with piled up work and an emotional meltdown on their part. It can even lead to an event falling apart with resulting embarrassment for the whole team. Leaders such as this will gain a reputation of being hard to work with. They will often go through a lot of new team members because everyone on their team quits after they have had enough of their leader's disorganized approach. Leadership is a big responsibility, and I believe that God wants us to take it seriously and truly honor people's time and commitments.

- Do have regularly scheduled meetings leading up to events and set deadlines for tasks to be completed. During those meetings check your timelines, hear reports and adjust assignments. This is where having strong team leaders and clear job descriptions is important. There should be a healthy tension between delegating and accountability. Good leadership structures and job descriptions that are paired together with accountability will make for successful outcomes. No one likes to be micromanaged. Ask your team if they feel micromanaged by you in any area. Conversely, ask them if they feel they have enough support as they complete their tasks. If you gain your team's help in developing their job descriptions, you will be able to see quickly which parts of the work you can let go of and which parts you need to supervise or do yourself.

- When it comes to timelines, do not launch your dream or give your product to the public too quickly. People need a level of certainty to buy into something, and if you do not know exactly what your dream is, then how can they? Your dream should be like an expanding circle that grows slowly out from the center where you pray and flesh out your *why*, your mission statement and the hard work to develop the foundation that will hold up the dream. That foundation includes all of the "Ts" that we have talked about over the last few chapters: tools, tasks, team, targets and timelines. A well-developed dream will be easy to articulate, and a sound vision will sell itself to people. If you try to put it out too soon, before you have completed the foundational work, it will be hard to snatch it back and make changes. When I was about a year into taking over as the director of Women on the Frontlines, I had a man tell me that he could get us a million followers on social media for a certain (expensive) cost. I prayed about it, but I could not find any peace about paying someone to get us followers. As I prayed, I realized that I did not want just a bunch of likes on Facebook. I wanted, instead, fully committed women who were truly interested in walking with Women on the Frontlines. To get that I would need to do the hard work to build the dream without any shortcuts. I would need to let God grow it organically. This is the best kind of growth for any business or ministry. I like to coach people to first master their dream themselves. Lose the weight, create and successfully use the product you invented or live out the lessons from the book you want to write. This will allow you to gain authority and confidence inside of yourself. Once that has happened, begin to invite a few friends to serve the dream with you and give you feedback about how it works for them. Use your team's feedback as you test market your dream or product. Run some free classes and get more feedback, if that applies. Take the time needed to work out the kinks, cut through the red tape and gain authority together. Then you will be ready to expand with confidence, to speak about your dream in a compelling way, to release your passion and to invite others to buy in. When you work with this natural progression, you will gain true converts and followers to your cause.

Questions for Journaling or Discussion

1. Most of us have experienced bad leadership at some point in our lives. What are the worst character traits that you have seen in a leader, and how did those traits have an impact on you?

2. What are the character traits you admire most in a good leader?

3. What are three characteristics that you have identified about the people you want to reach with your dream?

4. What are five core values that you carry that you would want to weave into a set of values for your team to live by?

5. How would you go about confronting a team member who is not showing up for meetings or following through on his or her commitment? What would be most important to you about the outcome of your meeting with your team member?

9

Taking Off the Limits, from Micro to Macro

Let your light shine before others,
so that they may see your good works.

Now that you have completed the chapters that have dealt with putting the "Ts" into your opportunity (tasks, tools, target, team and timelines), you have done much of the practical work necessary to lay out a blueprint for success. Taking the time to work though those steps is absolutely essential for the success of your dream, for if you move too fast and do not build your foundation correctly, your foundation may not be able to sustain the expansion that God has planned for your dream.

Do you know that God may have more planned for your dream than you do? In fact, in every dream I have worked on, there came a point where I realized that God's vision for what I was doing was bigger than I could have imagined initially. This should not surprise us, because the Bible tells us that God can do more that we can even imagine. "Now to him who is able to do far more abundantly than all that we ask or think, according to the power at work within us, to him be glory in the church and in Christ Jesus throughout all generations, forever and ever" (Ephesians 3:20–21).

I would like to ask you to take a moment and think about what could happen with your dream if there were no limits on where it could go. How big could it be? How many people could it have an impact on? And ask yourself a deeper question. Is there any way that you have limited your vision for what God can do with your dream?

Why ask that question now, while the dream is so small? Simply because it is essential to build your foundation with future growth in mind. If God has planted within you a capacity to shine and share your dream with many, it will be important that you build accordingly and surrender to the process by which God takes your dream from small to big—or as this chapter says, from micro to macro.

In the Scripture passage from Matthew that we have been studying, Jesus said, "In the same way, let your light shine before others, so that they may see your good works" (Matthew 5:16). This is a reminder that the purpose of positioning our light is so that people will see our good works, which will point to God's Kingdom. God may take your dream from micro to macro so that through it more people can see His love and His Kingdom.

Esteem or reward, however, is no greater for being used by God on a larger platform than it is for being used by God on a smaller platform. God knows what He has placed in each of us, and in some people He places a capacity to increase the reach of the light they carry to the point that the light greatly influences others and creates cultural transformation. For those who have a greater reach, they typically do not set out with that as their goal, but it is sometimes where they find themselves. God can use our lives in unprecedented ways. Sometimes those ways are hidden to us until it is time for those plans to be revealed. We may remain hidden until the moment that His preparation within us for that unprecedented season, action or moment has been completed. Consider the opportunity that God is positioning you for in your dream. Could there be more to come than you have seen up until this moment?

This is exactly what happened to me in my journey with God and Women on the Frontlines. I started out with a simple desire to shine my light to encourage and empower women to whatever degree God wanted to use me. I had lost any desire for fame or notoriety years before, and I was simply enjoying the journey with Women on the Frontlines and the fruit it was bearing.

In the spring of 2019, Patricia King took the first steps to pass the reins of the global ministry to me with a formal commissioning at one of our national events. During my commissioning I was charged by Patricia to seek God for the future of the ministry. And while it is true that I had been asking God for an expanded vision, for the most part, I could only envision that as creating a slightly bigger version of what Women on the Frontlines had been for many years—a ministry that hosted women's events.

That is until God turned my world upside down on September 15, 2019, through a spiritual encounter that would change the trajectory of my life and that of Women on the Frontlines. One spiritual practice I use that is a regular part of my relationship with God is going on prayer walks. I find that getting out of the house and away from distractions so that I can fully focus on God is beneficial to my spiritual growth. On the day mentioned, I went on one of those two-hour prayer walks. The day had been nothing out of the ordinary. I was simply walking along and praying in the Spirit. Suddenly, however, I found myself encountering a rarefied atmosphere of God's presence, which was thick around me.

In that moment, God began to speak to my heart and made me aware that I was not only standing on the shoulders of the women who had founded Women on the Frontlines, but I was standing on their lives and deaths. One of those women was Michal Ann Goll, who had launched and served the ministry in the early years. She had died prematurely while working to help women find their places and voices as never before. As I encountered God's presence that day, it was as if Michal Ann was right there before me. The knowledge of this reality and the feeling of being singled out as the next carrier of this ministry communicated to me clearly that I was receiving a holy commission that had been paid for with women's lives. I felt humbled and challenged not to take lightly the opportunity God had given me.

As I encountered the Lord on my walk that day in the thick atmosphere of His presence, He brought to my mind the Bible story of the wedding banquet to which the master invited many guests. The people he invited, however, were reluctant to come because they were too busy with their lives.

> "Tell those who are invited, 'See, I have prepared my dinner, my oxen and my fat calves have been slaughtered, and everything is ready. Come to the wedding feast.' But they paid no attention and went off, one to his farm, another to his business."
>
> Matthew 22:4–5

He showed me that women's ministry events had become like the wedding banquet. In many cases, the women we were preparing for were too busy to come. Rather than increasing in numbers, our ministry conferences were starting to draw lower numbers. What had worked in the past for Women on the Frontlines would not work as well in this current season.

As I continued to pray and ponder what God was revealing to me, He magnified to me the concluding verses of the above story in Matthew.

> "'Go therefore to the main roads and invite to the wedding feast as many as you find.' And those servants went out into the roads and gathered all whom they found, both bad and good. So the wedding hall was filled with guests."
>
> Matthew 22:9–10

God showed me through these verses that He was calling me to take Women on the Frontlines from an events ministry that ministered primarily inside the church and turn its focus outward "to the main roads." We were to be used to bring in the great harvest of souls during this next season. That instruction would have felt quite doable and fine, but then I heard God's voice at the conclusion of this encounter say something staggering. While I did not hear an audible voice, what I heard in my heart was so big, so unexpected and so outside of my expectations that I stopped walking, I stopped praying, and I stood utterly still and shocked. These words reverberated through my mind and heart: *Ask Me for a million women and I will give them to you.*

A million women?

Hey God, I think you missed the memo that I was hidden until I was fifty. Not to mention that I have no idea how to gather a million women or the fact that this kind of public exposure is way beyond anything that I thought I had signed up for or felt qualified to handle. Yes, I had big dreams and visions about ministry when I was younger, but we both know that I am too old to be getting started on such a big assignment. Right, God? Hello? Are you listening?

But the encounter was over, and the thick spiritual presence had dissipated. I spent the rest of my walk trying to understand what had happened and, to a certain degree, tried to talk myself out of it. In fact, by the time I arrived at home, all I could think was, *It would be really embarrassing if I were to tell people that I am to gather a million people and then fail at it.*

You can imagine my shock when, right after I walked in the door, I opened my Facebook page to do some ministry updates only to have the first post I laid my eyes on be a photo of Michal Ann Goll's gravestone. Her husband, James Goll, had written in the caption, "Visited Dover Cemetery this afternoon where Michal Ann is buried. September 15th is the 11th Anniversary of her Home-going."[1] If you remember, Michal Ann was the woman who had started the Women on the Frontlines ministry alongside her husband James. God had spoken to my heart that I was standing on the lives and deaths of those who had gone before me with Women on the Frontlines.

God was not going to let me escape this encounter. My spiritual encounter in which I received the million-woman mandate happening on the exact anniversary of Michal Ann's departure to heaven was the first of many confirmations that God brought to pass over the next few months. It was being made clear to me that God had invited me to ask Him for a million women, and this was going to be the next step of my journey—even though this part of His plan had been largely hidden from me up until this point. He was taking the reach of my light from micro to macro and was preparing me to lead a movement of women at a specific moment in history.

We can see this same journey in the lives of many in the Bible, but particularly in the life of Moses. Moses, like many of us, had found himself growing older yet not having fulfilled the big dream God had given him when he was younger. That dream was to stop the injustice against his people, the Israelites, who had been held captive in Egypt for hundreds of years. Like me, Moses had been hidden. He had been living out in the desert for forty years, seemingly doing one thing—shepherding sheep. A small job, a hidden job, but something he had mastered over those years. He was a qualified shepherd, and he knew how to use his staff. In fact, his staff was the tool of his trade. It was a symbol of the skill set that he had used up until this time.

In the book of Exodus, we have a window into the moment when God called Moses (as He will call some of us) to move from doing what he knew on a micro scale to allowing God to bring that skill set into play in a much larger, macro scale of impact. God took him from shepherding a flock of sheep to shepherding two million people into their destiny. Exodus chapter 3 starts out with the story of Moses encountering a burning bush and receiving God's instructions to go to Pharaoh to demand that he let the Israelites go. In this moment, Moses is not only receiving an assignment to put his light on display on a public stage, but he is being asked to revisit the dream that he failed at as a young man. This dream had been hidden under a basket for forty years.

> Then the LORD said, "I have surely seen the affliction of my people who are in Egypt and have heard their cry because of their taskmasters. I know their sufferings, and I have come down to deliver them out of the hand of the Egyptians and to bring them up out of that land to a good and broad land, a land flowing with milk and honey, to the place of the Canaanites, the Hittites, the Amorites, the Perizzites, the Hivites, and the Jebusites. And now, behold, the cry of the people of Israel has come to me, and I have also seen the oppression with which the Egyptians oppress them. Come, I will send you to Pharaoh that you may bring my people, the children of Israel, out of Egypt."
>
> Exodus 3:7–10

What follows in the life of Moses is an identity crisis, in spite of the fact that God had reassured him that He would be with him. When he was confronted with the big new assignment that God gave him, he said:

> "Who am I that I should go to Pharaoh and bring the children of Israel out of Egypt?" He said, "But I will be with you, and this shall be the sign for you, that I have sent you: when you have brought the people out of Egypt, you shall serve God on this mountain."
>
> Exodus 3:11–12

Then, in chapter 4, we find Moses responding to this great big assignment much as I did when I thought about gathering a million women. "Oh boy, it's too big. No one will listen to me, and it will be really embarrassing if it fails."

> Then Moses answered, "But behold, they will not believe me or listen to my voice, for they will say, 'The LORD did not appear to you.'" The LORD said to him, "What is that in your hand?" He said, "A staff." And he said, "Throw it on the ground." So he threw it on the ground, and it became a serpent, and Moses ran from it.
>
> Exodus 4:1–3

What I want to look at specifically is the story of Moses' staff and what God asked him to do. He asked Moses to cast down his staff. As Moses did that, it turned into a snake, and he ran from it. This is such a good picture of what happens to us when God wants to change our skill set from micro to macro, from shining our light a little to shining it really big. The skill set that we hold in our hand has been effective in the small ways that God has called us to use it. In my case, I had been shepherding women effectively for years in small ways, in small groups and on small stages. But that skill set had to be released, thrown down and transformed, because it would not work in that micro model to create a movement of women one million strong.

I had to throw down everything that I knew about women's ministry. As God's power hit, He called me into the million-woman mandate and asked me to go public with it. Building a big charity that would reach around the globe would require me to travel almost full-time, to be constantly in the spotlight and to confront the pharaohs of this age. And like Moses, as I saw the very thing that I thought I knew (women's ministry) cast down and transitioning into the new mandate to which God was calling me look like a big, frightening thing. All I wanted to do was run away from it. I felt scared and intimidated by the new the assignment God had given me. It was moving and changing to the point that what I thought I had signed up for with Women on the Frontlines was no longer recognizable to me. And in reality, that is exactly what was happening.

Transition looks like movement. It makes what we know look unrecognizable as God changes it into what is needed in our next season. It takes what we hold in our hand, our basic skill set, such as Moses' staff, and changes it into a powerful weapon to defeat the enemy on a wider scale than we had ever imagined.

Two Things Needed

This transition from micro to macro requires two things from us. Let's look at them.

Number one: This transition requires that we are willing to lay down the skill set that we know and surrender it fully to God. God said to Moses, "What is in your hand? Now cast it down." He will say the same to us in the process of moving our dreams from micro to macro.

God may say, *Take everything you think you know about how to do things and cast it down. The form it is in now—the way you think about it, interact with it, all that is dear to you in the way it has been built—will not work for what is next. Cast that down and let it go, for I am about to transform it into something that you will not recognize. It will be so unrecognizable that you will want to run from it at first.*

This letting go can be painful. It requires humility and the crucifying of our ego. After all, we have built something to a certain size and we have mastered it, so to cast that down is no easy task. As God worked this transition in my life, I suddenly felt as if I was back at the starting gate. Instead of feeling experienced and competent, as I had for years, I now felt inexperienced, incompetent and intimidated—just to name a few emotions that came with the transition.

These same fears and feelings are what keep many organizations from major growth. They cling to outdated ways of doing things simply due to sentimentality, fear of change or not wanting to feel out of control and incompetent in front of others who currently see them as experts.

Transition looks like movement. It makes what we know look unrecognizable as God changes it into what is needed in our next season.

Yet God requires us to let go completely if we are going to move our dream from micro to macro. This means a number of necessary endings will come into play. You may need to cast down the structure of how your business or ministry works, and that may involve ending some positions, opening up new ones or letting go of an old target for your light and embracing a new one. This points to the second thing God needs from us to take us from micro to macro.

Number two: We must get past our fear of the transformed call God has for us and take hold of the new opportunity He is offering. Notice what God said to Moses about his fear of the staff:

> But the LORD said to Moses, "Put out your hand and catch it by the tail"—so he put out his hand and caught it, and it became a staff in his hand—"that they may believe that the LORD, the God of their fathers, the God of Abraham, the God of Isaac, and the God of Jacob, has appeared to you."
>
> Exodus 4:4–5

God was saying to Moses, "Reach out and take this by the tail—by the least scary point of contact—and as you do that it will transform into a tool that you can handle, a tool that you recognize. You've got this, Moses. You are still a shepherd, and you know what to do. You know how to lead, and you know how to move groups across this desert. Only now you are going to do it on a big scale. In this transformed skill set, this staff will become the rod of God, the conduit of God's power and authority for this moment in history."

So that is what I did. I reached out toward this scary new million-women mandate for Women on the Frontlines, and I picked it up by the least scary point of contact I could see and began to work on it. As Moses did, I was now carrying something that was way beyond my comfort zone in terms of what I knew, but also way beyond anything I had ever known in its power and potential to have an impact on the world.

I remember Joan Hunter praying over me during my commissioning as the Director for Women on the Frontlines and saying, "I have a real simple word for you. If you knew you could do it, it would not be God."[2] Little did I know how true those words would prove to be!

If you recognize yourself in this chapter, remember that, like Moses, Esther, me and many others, God often calls us into the Kingdom for a certain moment in time, for a certain assignment or to a certain people. The uncovering of that call can happen in a moment. On September 14, 2019, my biggest assignment and capacity were hidden within me. Then on September 15, they were revealed.

If you are just getting started on your first dream, do not worry at all about going from micro to macro. Just begin to work on your dream, build with excellence and go as far as you can. Only God knows where the sweet spot will be for each of us, and He may keep what you are building a certain size because that is the size and place that will give you the most joy and allow your light to have the greatest impact on others.

I have even seen the opposite from what I described in this chapter in play. People with smaller assignments can become so obsessed with big that they do not produce much fruit where they are presently. Like a spotlight that is always pointed up at the sky, they forget to give their light to the people right in their house. They live never satisfied and never quite content, not understanding that God has not called us to exposure but to effectiveness. And so they end up with nothing but an empty soul attached to fame, and God not being the one directing it.

If God is calling you to transition something you have built from micro to macro, I want you to understand the process of the staff. If that is you, I invite you to let go and to cast down what you think you know and what you have built. Do not be afraid to allow it to change into something unrecognizable or a little scary in its new form, knowing that it has a great and powerful purpose for its next season. Then, once you have let go of what you know, do not let intimidation stop you. Grab that unrecognizable assignment by the tail—the least intimidating spot—and go for it. Do what you can do, and God will do what you cannot.

Following my spiritual encounter with God on September 15, 2019, I had to reframe what I saw for the future of Women on the Frontlines and begin to see it through God's eyes. I had to find a place where I could reach out, pick up the dream and begin to work toward the vast new goal that God had given me.

Since the time of that encounter, I have done things I had never imagined I would do. I have launched charities in two countries, built an online media presence with multiple shows each week, managed a large international team of seventeen women and sought the Lord together with that team for the future of Women on the Frontlines. Together we are positioning ourselves to fulfill the words, "Go therefore to the main roads and invite to the wedding feast as many as you find" (Matthew 22:9). I firmly believe that what God has done for me He will also do for you as you become willing to cast down your staff and courageously make the transition from micro to macro.

What else can you take away from this chapter? I want you to be encouraged by the thought that God does not place big dreams within us to torment us. I also want you to recognize that we cannot position ourselves in our own strength to do the really big things that He has destined for us before His timing is revealed. But if you will take the limits off and be willing to be used by Him in outstanding ways, you can rest knowing that you have aligned yourself for maximum effectiveness during your time on earth. At any moment, God can take you into that next place of destiny and influence through what He has planned for you to let your light shine before others so that they may see your good works.

Questions for Journaling or Discussion

1. When you think about the idea of God taking your dream from micro to macro, what do you picture? How big is it, and who is it having an impact on?

2. What aspect of your skill set that you carry currently (your staff) would need to change drastically if God called your dream to have a global reach?

3. What would be the drawbacks of having your dream be ten times the size of what you are imagining now?

4. What would be the positive impact on the world around you that would come from receiving a call to make your dream really big?

10

Do Not Forget What Matters Most

Give glory to your Father
who is in heaven.

As we conclude our time together, I feel much like a mother who is standing at the door of her home as she sends her adult child off on a journey into his or her dreams and future, knowing she can only watch from a distance. I want to call out, "Drive carefully" or "Keep an eye on the weather" and other such overused platitudes that simply reflect every mother's worry of whether she has done everything she can to prepare her child for the journey ahead.

And while I am certainly not your natural mother, I have held you in my heart as a spiritual mother as I have written this book and prayed for its impact on your life to be fruitful. So I do have a sense of that same question in my heart as I consider whether there are any final words of wisdom that I need to convey to you. As I ponder this, there are two things that come to mind that I want to call out to you as you are setting out on your journey. The first is to beware of the dream killers, and the second is to not forget what matters the most.

Beware of the Dream Killers

If you look around, I am sure that you will see that there are many more people who launch dreams than there are people who finish them. And while enthusiasm and confidence are high at the beginning of every dream, somewhere along the journey something happens that causes many people to give up and fail to complete what God has put into their heart. The dream killers sneak in along the way and steal the focus and confidence of the dreamer.

Like that mother who is standing at the door and cheering you on as you launch into your journey, I do not want that to happen to you. I want you to take seriously my words "Beware of the dream killers," because I want you to make it all the way through to the finish line with your dream. And while the dream killers may be lurking along the pathway of your journey toward success, once you know how to recognize them, you can also learn how to confidently move past them.

The Bible teaches us about dream killers in the book of Mark. We read about the parable of the sower that Jesus first taught and then interpreted to His disciples. As you read through both the parable and Jesus' interpretation, I want you to think about your dream as the word that God has sown as a seed into your heart. Your heart is the soil where your dream grows, and the condition of your heart can either cause your dream to thrive or fail. Let's look at the parable of the sower to understand this better:

"Listen! Behold, a sower went out to sow. And as he sowed, some seed fell along the path, and the birds came and devoured it. Other seed fell on rocky ground, where it did not have much soil, and immediately it sprang up, since it had no depth of soil. And when the sun rose, it was scorched, and since it had no root, it withered away. Other seed fell among thorns, and the thorns grew up and choked it, and it yielded no grain. And other seeds fell into good soil and produced grain, growing up and increasing and yielding thirtyfold and sixtyfold and a hundredfold." And he said, "He who has ears to hear, let him hear."

Mark 4:3–9

Now let's look at Jesus' interpretation of the parable to see if you can recognize the dream killers that try to take the seed of your dream from you. I have placed the word *dream* in brackets throughout this Scripture passage to help you see its application. Jesus said in His explanation of the parable:

"The sower sows the word [of your dream]. And these are the ones along the path, where the word [dream] is sown: when they hear [about the dream that God has for them], Satan immediately comes and takes away the word [dream] that is sown in them. And these are the ones sown on rocky ground: the ones who, when they hear the word [dream], immediately receive it with joy. And they have no root in themselves, but endure for a while; then, when tribulation or persecution arises on account of the word [dream], immediately they fall away. And others are the ones sown among thorns. They are those who hear the word [dream], but the cares of the world and the deceitfulness of riches and the desires for other things enter in and choke the word [dream], and it proves unfruitful. But those that were sown on the good soil are the ones who hear the word [of their dream] and accept it and bear fruit, thirtyfold and sixtyfold and a hundredfold."

Mark 4:14–20

The Dream Killer Called Doubt

The first dream killer that appears in this story is doubt. Notice that Jesus said that the word (of your dream) is sown, but Satan comes immediately to steal the word from you. Ask yourself an important question. How many great ideas have come to you over the years that you have immediately dismissed because of doubt? Probably a lot. Doubt keeps you from accepting the vision of your upgraded future in God. Doubt has a voice that says, "What if this goes wrong, or what if _____ happens?" The voice of doubt will continue to throw *what ifs* at you until you either give up the dream or learn to move past the voice of doubt. I want to encourage you to be prepared to deal with doubt rather than being surprised by it.

See it as a hurdle that you will likely encounter in the first season of your dream. Learn to recognize it and call it what it is. "Oh, here are some thoughts of doubt attacking my dream." Then deal with the doubt and keep moving. The purpose of the dream killer of doubt is to steal your dream while it is still in a seed form before it even takes root. Determine from the beginning that you will deal with doubt immediately and decisively.

First of all, hold on to your dream when it comes to you, and do not let it be snatched away. Make sure that you write it down in an easily accessible format. All through Scripture, God tells His people to write down anything of importance. In the book of Habakkuk, the prophet recorded these words, "Then the LORD answered me and said, 'Write down the vision and inscribe it clearly on tablets, so that one who reads it may run'" (Habakkuk 2:2 NASB).

In this instance, Habakkuk was referring to writing down the word so that a courier could take the news and run with it to all the places it needed to go. In your case, it means writing down the dream God has given you so you can run with it. For if you have done the work outlined in this book, you will have your *why*, your purpose and much more in written form. And this blueprint that you have created for your dream will help you immensely when it comes to dealing with doubt.

Whenever you are hit with doubt, the fastest way to defeat it is by reminding yourself of the "God has said" statements. That is how you snatch your dream back from the dream killer of doubt. In my life, this means that I review the mission statement I have written for my dream. I review the promises from the Bible that I believe speak to my vision, and I review any prophetic words or significant prayers people have spoken over me that relate to my dream. I take those words, and I declare them out loud regularly, using them to frame the image of my dream and call it into being. Do not let doubt be a dream killer that steals the seed of your dream before you even get moving. Rather, see it as a necessary obstacle that is attached to every dream, and one that you are more than able to move past and defeat as you continue along your way.

The Dream Killer Called Discouragement

This dream killer appears once you have said yes to your dream and have moved past the test of doubt. You are no longer questioning whether the dream is real or whether you can do it. Your dream is beginning to grow into a beautiful seedling, and you are starting to see its potential come forth. But with every dream comes a cost that is necessary to bring the dream to pass. If God has called you to be a world changer, that means you are going to change things, and some people are not going to like the changes you bring. They are going to oppose your dream, or even persecute you.

Jesus explained it this way:

> "And these are the ones sown on rocky ground: the ones who, when they hear the word, immediately receive it with joy. And they have no root in themselves, but endure for a while; then, when tribulation or persecution arises on account of the word, immediately they fall away."
>
> Mark 4:16–17

Notice it says that "they have no root in themselves." In the beginning season of a dream, it may not be rooted deeply in the right things. It is often rooted in your belief in your own strength or in people's opinions and ideas instead of full confidence in God. In fact, the Greek word for *fall away* that is used in this parable is *skandalizó*. This translates to "become entrapped, ensnared and offended by something."[1] This dream killer operates by causing you to become offended and ensnared by the words of those who reject or oppose your dream, which in turn leads to deep discouragement. Yet this is a redemptive process if you understand that every dream must move from being rooted in your opinion and strength and other people's opinions to being rooted deeply in God's opinion, God's love, God's blueprint and His strength, love and daily directions for you.

The way to defeat this dream killer is to hold tight to your vision and cling to God in the face of opposition and persecution. Persecution and opposition act as sifting forces to help you decide why you believe in your dream. This forces you to go deeper with God, to develop your trust in Him and to confirm your certainty that He has called you into the dream and is with you in the dream. It forces you to pray until the point that you can hold on to the dream in the face of any opposition, just as Jesus did with His divine assignment on earth.

If you do not understand this process, however, you can easily let the dream killer of discouragement come in and steal your dream. Opposition is not fun, and neither is persecution. It can feel isolating. You might even lose team members who will leave you high and dry as soon as any opposition comes because they are not deeply rooted in the dream.

I have gone through a season of discouragement in every one of my dreams. Because I am a change agent and a forerunner, it is easy for people to oppose the change I am bringing because it threatens the comfortable places where things are. Over the years, I have endured opposition, been deeply misunderstood and judged, and even had a full-on slander campaign released against me.

Yet in looking back I can see that each of these difficult experiences ultimately strengthened my dreams and rooted them deeply in the soil of God's love, God's wisdom and the certainty that He was with me. The opposition I experienced forced me to fight for the dream and pay the price for it to come to maturity, which led to receiving God's divine blueprint and direction on how to move forward. This will prove to be true for you, too, as long as you do not allow the dream killer of discouragement to steal your dreams by causing you to become offended or give up.

I have a couple of keys that I want to share with you for dealing with this dream killer. The first is to understand that every dream has a dose of opposition and persecution attached to it that must be overcome in order to mature the dream. You do not need to go looking for opposition and persecution, but you should not be surprised when it shows up. Understand that it has a redemptive purpose, and ask God to root you deeply into His love, wisdom and partnership during that season. Keep a close watch on your heart during times of opposition, walk in love and forgive those who reject your dream. Remind yourself that it is not their dream, so of course they do not understand it.

The second key is to surround yourself with loyal friends who will dream for you on the difficult days, who will remind you of who you are and what God has called you to do and who will not allow you to quit due to discouragement. If you have team members who abandon you in this season, remember that this is part of the redemptive sifting of the dream. God is strengthening the dream and removing things in this season that do not belong in its future.

The Dream Killer Called Distraction

This is the dream killer that sneaks in to choke the fruit of your dream once it starts to become established. It shows up after you have defeated the dream killers of doubt and discouragement and you are on your way to success. I call this dream killer distraction because it comes in to take your focus off of God and off of the primary focus of your mission, and it places it somewhere it does not belong.

Jesus said it this way: "And others are the ones sown among thorns. They are those who hear the word, but the cares of the world and the deceitfulness of riches and the desires for other things enter in and choke the word, and it proves unfruitful" (Mark 4:18–19).

This is a powerful warning not to allow your focus to become distracted from your core mission and your relationship with God by placing it onto other things that can choke the life of your dream, therefore causing it to be unfruitful. Have you ever seen a minister who was very gifted, but something was off in the way the minister handled money? Or perhaps you have met someone with a business dream who was so consumed with worry that they were not enjoying the journey at all.

In each case, the dream was being choked by a wrong focus, so it was not fully fruitful. The parable identifies several things we need to be aware of that can pull our eyes off of a right focus and steal our dream. These include cares and worries, a focus on money, and lust for other things, which I believe includes the lust for power, position and possessions. All of these things can become distractions and cause our dream to be less fruitful. I have found that the best way for me to deal with these dream killing distractions is to live authentically and humbly before God and others who offer me accountability.

I have a group of people in my life that I have given permission to correct me and speak into my life if they see me get out of balance or full of myself. This group starts with my own family and includes carefully chosen mentors and guides. They notice quickly if I have become overburdened or worried, and they can detect pridefulness or other sins due to their long journey with me. The most dangerous leader is a leader who does not have accountability. Most leaders start out with an accountability team, but as their success increases, they believe the lie that they no longer require the same level of support and relationship that they had in the beginning.

Do not let that happen to you. Ensure that you build into your schedule regular meetings with your accountability team, and do not wait until something is going terribly wrong to involve them in your life. Taking this proactive approach has helped me to deal with issues while they are small. I also attend a personal healing prayer session or retreat at least once a year where anything that needs to be dealt with in my heart can be brought to the surface.

How about you? What kind of distractions are you likely to be susceptible to along the way? Think about it before you take too many steps on the road to success, and you will be well prepared for the dream killer that is called distraction.

The Completed Dream

The parable ends with the story of those who completed the dream and produced thirty, sixty or one hundred times what was sown into their hearts. The Scripture passage says they heard the word, accepted it and bore much fruit. They heard the word of their dream from God, they got past the hurdle of doubt, they accepted the dream and they overcame discouragement. Their roots went deep, and they did not give in to distraction, so they were fruitful.

I know you want to be like the people in the parable who were the most fruitful with their dreams. As we close this chapter, imagine once again that you are standing on the sidewalk outside of your home preparing to leave on the journey toward your dream. As your spiritual mom, I have been standing in the doorway telling you to beware of the dream killers. As we have looked at them together, my hope is that you feel a bit more prepared for what lies along the road ahead. Yet in my heart, I want to leave you with some final words that you will remember above all else and can come back to again and again no matter what happens along the way.

With this in mind, my final advice to you in this book and as you prepare to take on your dream is simply this: Do not forget what matters most.

Do Not Forget What Matters Most

As I have pondered what to say to you as we conclude our journey together, I have realized that no matter what we discuss, it all comes down to one simple thing: God and you in relationship together. That is it. If you accomplish your dream without God, you may have the world, but your soul will remain empty. And God has made it clear throughout the Bible that while

He is the all-knowing, all-powerful, all-present Creator of the universe, His life is not complete unless you are in it. You are truly that important to Him.

Let's look back now at the complete passage in Matthew that we have been studying throughout this book and how it relates to what I am saying:

> "You are the salt of the earth, but if salt has lost its taste, how shall its saltiness be restored? It is no longer good for anything except to be thrown out and trampled under people's feet. You are the light of the world. A city set on a hill cannot be hidden. Nor do people light a lamp and put it under a basket, but on a stand, and it gives light to all in the house. In the same way, let your light shine before others, so that they may see your good works and give glory to your Father who is in heaven."
>
> Matthew 5:13–16

Did you notice where Jesus put the focus of His words? The focus is on you. *You* are the salt, *you* are the light, let *your* light shine so that people see *your* good works. So often I have heard it taught in church that "it is not about you." This subtly shaming message that perhaps is intended to keep people humble has only contributed to keeping people's light dimmed and their gifts hidden.

Jesus said here that it is about you. It is so much about you that Jesus told many stories in the gospels that were focused on changing people's perception of how the Father viewed them and valued them. Stories such as the one in the gospel of Luke about the shepherd who left the 99 sheep to rescue the one lost sheep. Or the story of the father who raced toward his broken failure of a prodigal son, threw his arms around him and wept for joy at his return. These stories reveal a Father who longs for relationship with you, and who invites you from

191

that relationship to partner with Him to shine your light and be a bridge to bring others to Him "so that they may see your good works and give glory to your Father who is in heaven" (Matthew 5:16).

This is the simplicity of the Gospel, and the real *why* for your dream that would still be there even if all of your other motivations were to fade away.

As I have studied the life and story of the apostle Paul throughout the New Testament, I have been amazed and challenged by what he had to say toward the conclusion of his life. For after everything he experienced, including his previous life as an educated and influential Roman citizen, through every miracle, triumph and disaster, through being shipwrecked and jailed and being lifted into one of the most powerful places of authority in the Church, he said these words:

> But whatever gain I had, I counted as loss for the sake of Christ. Indeed, I count everything as loss because of the surpassing worth of knowing Christ Jesus my Lord. For his sake I have suffered the loss of all things and count them as rubbish, in order that I may gain Christ and be found in him.
>
> Philippians 3:7–9

The most important thing to Paul after every dream he had pursued and after every triumph and every trial was knowing Jesus and being found in Him.

When your life is almost complete and you look back on everything that you have had and everything that you have done during your journey on the earth, there will be one thing that really matters. That is the answer to these questions: Did you try your best to do what God put in your heart, and did you live your life for Him? This is really all that matters in the end. Your possessions will not mean much, and neither will any fame you have achieved.

When I would visit my father-in-law in his nursing home, the only difference I could see between one resident or another was not the cost of the reclining chair in their little room, but the number of visitors they had. I could only guess that this was because of how the residents had either lived their lives for others or had lived their lives for themselves. And when I visited my sister a week before she died, I had nothing that I could give her that would improve her life. All she wanted to talk about was eternity.

If you accomplish your dream without God, you may have the world, but your soul will remain empty.

And that is what I want to leave you with. The single most important thing I want you to hold on to is that when it has all been said and done, your dream is simply a pathway by which you walk into the arms and heart of your loving Father. Your light is only as glorious as your love for Him, and as long as you have done your best to live for that, your dream will be a success.

It Is Your Time to Shine

Whether you are 20 years old and just starting out, or 65 years old and just getting started, this is your time to shine! There has never been a better moment for you to launch your dream and live the life you have been waiting for. God has been stirring you, inspiring you and positioning your heart as you have read this book. He is calling to you, and all He needs is your simple yes. It is never too late for you to be what you might have been, and it is never too late to get started.

I want to challenge you to go further than just allowing this book to be another self-help, informational volume that gets read and put aside. I want to end by inviting you to give your yes to God's invitation to partner with Him and launch your dream right now. Can you do that? Can you find the courage to say yes to the dream of God? I believe you can, and I invite you to pray this prayer out loud and to make a commitment to see it through.

Father in heaven, I am making a decision to say yes to the dream that You have placed in my heart. I understand that the most important things that I can do with my life are to shine my light through activating my dream and to draw others to You. I am making a decision today to choose courage over fear and to step out in faith to pursue everything that You have for me to accomplish in my lifetime. I understand there may be opposition to my dream and hurdles to overcome, but I am willing with Your help to stay committed to my dream and to You until together we see it come to fruition. I invite You to lead and guide me one step at a time through every stage of my dream and to give me the wisdom to implement all of the strategies and practical solutions I have learned through this book and through my own life experiences. In Jesus' name, Amen.

It has been an honor and a privilege to take this journey with you and dream together. It is my prayer that the lessons of this book be sown deep into your heart and bring forth a powerful and compelling dream beyond what you could have imagined. No matter what your age, stage of life or circumstance, I pray that you and your dream will be positioned to shine your light with such radiance that all who are in your house will turn to God and glorify Him when they see what He has done for you.

Over the years that I have been coaching women and men into their dreams, I have received many emails, photos and letters from people who have had their dreams come true after acting on what they learned. I would love to hear your feedback and the story of your journey into your dream. You can use the contact form at www.wendypeter.com or www.wofl.org to reach me with your testimony.

Questions for Journaling or Discussion

1. We talked about the dream killers called doubt, discouragement and distraction in this chapter. Try to identify any messages or strategies the dream killers are using to try to hinder your dream in each area. Go back to the strategies for defeating each dream killer and make note of what you need to do.

   - Doubt
   - Discouragement
   - Distraction

2. What is the legacy you would like to leave behind? In other words, what would you want said of you at your memorial service one day?

3. What are three things you need to commit to from your task list that you can get started on right now in order to get your dream moving forward?

4. What is your biggest takeaway from this book?

Notes

Chapter 1 From Hidden to Visible

1. Bible Hub, s.v. "5457.phos," accessed March 29, 2021, https://biblehub .com/greek/5457.htm.

2. Henry David Thoreau, *Walden* (New York: Thomas Y. Crowell and Company, 1910), 8.

3. Oxford Learner's Dictionaries, s.v. "crisis," accessed March 29, 2021, https://www.oxfordlearnersdictionaries.com/us/definition/english/crisis _1?q=crisis.

4. Blue Letter Bible, s.v. "krisis" (Strong's 2920), accessed March 29, 2021, https://www.blueletterbible.org/lang/lexicon/lexicon.cfm?t=kjv&strongs =g2920.

Chapter 2 Your Destined Place

1. Steven Furtick, "Crushing: God Turns Pressure into Power with Bishop T.D. Jakes & Pastor Steven Furtick," YouTube, April 12, 2019, https://www .youtube.com/watch?v=CzP23Zti-YI.

2. Michelle Lindsey, "Seeds from the Tombs," Homestead on the Range, May 23, 2017, https://homesteadontherange.com/2017/05/23/seeds-from-the -tombs/.

3. Andrew Curry, "Dead Sea Dates Grown From 2000-Year-Old-Seeds," *Science*, February 5, 2020, https://www.sciencemag.org/news/2020/02/dead -sea-dates-grown-2000-year-old-seeds.

4. Mac Lucado, *God Thinks You're Wonderful!* (Nashville: W Publishing, 2003), 56–66.

Chapter 3 Moments of Lift

1. David K. Li, "Sully: My Whole Life Was for This," *New York Post*, February 9, 2009, https://nypost.com/2009/02/09/sully-my-whole-life-was -for-this.
2. Jan Frank, *The Door of Hope* (Nashville: Thomas Nelson, 1995).

Chapter 4 Defining Your Dream

1. Philip W. Comfort and Walter A. Elwell, ed., *Tyndale Bible Dictionary* (Wheaton, IL: Tyndale House, 2001), 797–798.
2. Wikipedia, s.v. "Matthew 5:13," last modified February 24, 2021, 11:31, https://en.wikipedia.org/wiki/Matthew_5:13.
3. Lance Wallnau and Bill Johnson, *Invading Babylon: The 7 Mountain Mandate* (Shippensburg, PA: Destiny Image, 2013), press description.

Chapter 5 Staging Your Comeback

1. Lexico, s.v. "courage," accessed March 29, 2021, https://www.lexico .com/en/definition/courage.
2. David Braun, "Courage," sermon preached at Rock Lake Bible Camp, July 1, 2018.
3. Donna Krueger, *Driving with the Light: My Spiritual Road Trip* (Kingdom Creativity Press, 2019).
4. Gerren Keith Gaynor, "Twitter Thread Inspiring Middle-Aged People to Share Their 'Big Breaks' Goes Viral," Fox News, January 9, 2020, https:// www.foxnews.com/lifestyle/viral-twitter-thread-middle-aged-people-share -their-big-breaks.
5. Thomson Reuters, "Arise Sir Tom Moore: Queen Elizabeth Knights 100-Year-Old Fundraising Captain," CBC News, July 17, 2020, https://www .cbc.ca/news/world/captain-tom-knighthood-queen-elizabeth-1.5653222.
6. Bible Study Tools, s.v. "peirazo" (Strong's 3985), accessed March 29, 2021, https://www.biblestudytools.com/lexicons/greek/nas/peirazo.html.
7. Bible Hub, s.v. "4137.pléroó," accessed March 29, 2021, https://biblehub .com/greek/4137.htm.
8. Bible Study Tools, s.v. "pneumatikos" (Strong's 4152), accessed March 29, 2021, https://www.biblestudytools.com/lexicons/greek/kjv/pneumatikos .html.

Chapter 6 Breaking Free and Shining Brightly

1. John C. Maxwell, *Failing Forward: Turning Mistakes into Stepping Stones for Success* (New York: Harper Collins Leadership, 2000), 18.
2. Erica R. Hendry, "7 Epic Fails Brought to You by the Genius Mind of Thomas Edison," *Smithsonian*, November 20, 2013, https://www.smithsonian mag.com/innovation/7-epic-fails-brought-to-you-by-the-genius-mind-of -thomas-edison-180947786/.

3. Henry Cloud, *Necessary Endings* (New York: HarperCollins, 2011), 8.

4. Cloud, *Necessary Endings*, 7.

5. Marianne Williamson, *A Return to Love: Reflections on the Principles of a Course in Miracles* (New York: HarperCollins, 1992), 190–191.

6. Wikipedia, s.v. "Clapham Sect," last modified February 28 2021, 02:58, https://en.wikipedia.org/wiki/Clapham_Sect.

7. Janet Porter, "Deborahs United" conference video, Generals International, July 18, 2020, https://www.generals.org/deborahs2020, 3:51.

8. Porter, "Deborahs United," 3:57:58.

Chapter 9 Taking Off the Limits, from Micro to Macro

1. James Goll, Facebook photo, September 14, 2019, https://www.facebook.com/jamesgollpage/photos/a.394458211831/10157377775706832.

2. Joan Hunter, "Commissioning," video, Women on the Frontlines Facebook page, June 11, 2019, https://www.facebook.com/groups/www.wofl.org/permalink/2297286780510823, 9:35.

Chapter 10 Do Not Forget What Matters Most

1. Bible Study Tools, s.v. "skandalizo" (Strong's 4624), accessed March 29, 2021, https://www.biblestudytools.com/lexicons/greek/nas/skandalizo.html.

Wendy Peter is the director of Women on the Frontlines Global Ministry and is a pastor at the Wave Church in Winnipeg. She is an inspiring communicator, life coach and teacher of the Word of God, and she writes books and courses for women that speak to the real issues and challenges that they encounter in their life journeys. She believes that we were created to live outside of fear and inside of our dreams, and everything that she does flows out of this belief. She has spent her life empowering others to break free from the limitations and beliefs that have held them back.

Whether she is standing in front of a crowd of women or stepping onto a train in a foreign nation, she tries to live each day connected, alive and unencumbered.

She is married to Murray and enjoys doing life with her adult children.

Personal Notes

Personal Notes

Personal Notes

Personal Notes

Personal Notes

Personal Notes

Personal Notes